ASE Correlated T

for

AUTOMOTIVE
CHASSIS SYSTEMS

8th Edition

James D. Halderman

Director of Product Management: Linea Rowe
Product Manager, Trades, Hospitality, & Careers:
Derril Trakalo
Senior Analyst, HE Global Content, Trades &
Hospitality: Tara Warrens
Analyst, HE Global Content, Careers & Professional:
Bridget Daly
Manager Content HE, Careers & Professional:
Jenifer Niles
Director, Digital Studio & Content Production:
Brian Hyland
Managing Content Producer: Jennifer Sargunar
Managing Producer, Teacher Education &
Careers: Autumn Benson

Content Producer (Team Lead):
Faraz Sharique Ali
Permissions Editor: Jenell Forschler
Cover Design: Carie Keller, SPi
Cover Credit: Courtesy of ASE;
Henrik5000/E+/Getty images
Full-Service Management and Composition:
Integra Software Service Pvt. Ltd.
Printer/Binder: LSC Communications, Inc.
Cover Printer: LSC Communications, Inc.
Text Font: Helvetica Neue LT W1G

1 2020

ISBN 10:   0-13-576434-3
ISBN 13: 978-0-13-576434-3

TABLE OF CONTENTS

We Support
Education Foundation

VIN Code

Meets ASE Task: (A1 through A8-A-2) P-1 Locate and interpret vehicle identification numbers.

Name _____ Date _____ Time on Task _____

Make/Model/Year _____ VIN _____ Evaluation: 4   3   2   1

- The first number or letter designates the **country of origin** = _____

1 = United States	6 = Australia	L = China	V = France
2 = Canada	8 = Argentina	R = Taiwan	W = Germany
3 = Mexico	9 = Brazil	S = England	X = Russia
4 = United States	J = Japan	T = Czechoslovakia	Y = Sweden
5 = United States	K = Korea	U = Romania	Z = Italy

- The model of the vehicle is commonly the fourth or fifth character. **Model?** _____

- The eighth character is often the engine code. (Some engines cannot be determined by the VIN number.) **Engine code:** _____

- The tenth character represents the year on all vehicles. See the following chart.

VIN Year Chart (The pattern repeats every 30 years.)   **Year?** _____

A = 1980/2010	J = 1988/2018	T = 1996/2026	4 = 2004/2034
B = 1981/2011	K = 1989/2019	V = 1997/2027	5 = 2005/2035
C = 1982/2012	L = 1990/2020	W = 1998/2028	6 = 2006/2036
D = 1983/2013	M = 1991/2021	X = 1999/2029	7 = 2007/2037
E = 1984/2014	N = 1992/2022	Y = 2000/2030	8 = 2008/2038
F = 1985/2015	P = 1993/2023	1 = 2001/2031	9 = 2009/2039
G = 1986/2016	R = 1994/2024	2 = 2002/2032	
H = 1987/2017	S = 1995/2025	3 = 2003/2033	

Vehicle Service History

Meets ASE Task: (A1 through A8-A-2) P-1 Research vehicle service information, vehicle service history and TSBs.

Name _____ **Date** _____ **Time on Task** _____

Make/Model/Year _____ **VIN** _____ **Evaluation: 4   3   2   1**

_____ **1.** Search vehicle history (check all that apply).

      _____ Computerized data base (electronic file if previous service work)

      _____ Files (hard copy of previous service work)

      _____ Customer information (verbal)

      _____ Other (describe) _____

_____ **2.** What electrical-related repairs have been performed in this vehicle? _____

_____

_____

_____

_____ **3.** From the information obtained, has the vehicle been serviced regularly?

      _____ Yes (describe the service intervals) _____

_____

_____

      _____ No (why?) _____

_____

_____ **4.** Based on the service history information, is the service record helpful? Why or why not? _____

_____

_____

Pearson

We Support
ASE | Education Foundation

Technical Service Bulletins

Meets ASE Task: (A1 through A8-A-2) P-1 Research vehicle service information, vehicle service history and TSBs.

Name _____ **Date** _____ **Time on Task** _____

Make/Model/Year _____ **VIN** _____ **Evaluation: 4 3 2 1**

_____ **1.** Technical service bulletins can be accessed through (check all that apply):

_____ Internet site(s), specify _____

_____ Paper bulletins, specify source _____

_____ CD ROM bulletins, specify source _____

_____ Other (describe) _____

_____ **2.** List all electrical-related technical service bulletins that pertain to the vehicle/engine being serviced.

Number	Description/Correction
_____	_____
_____	_____
_____	_____
_____	_____

_____ **3.** Based on this research, is the information located helpful?

_____ Yes, why? _____

_____ No, why not? _____

We Support

Education Foundation

Service Information

Meets ASE Task: (A1-A-2) P-1 Research vehicle and service information, vehicle history and TSBs.

Name _____ **Date** _____ **Time on Task** _____

Make/Model/Year _____ **VIN** _____ **Evaluation: 4   3   2   1**

Look up the following service information and record the page number or document number where the information was found.

Spark plug number: _____ location found _____

Spark plug gap: _____ location found _____

Number of quarts of oil for an oil change: _____ location found _____

Viscosity of engine oil recommended: _____ location found _____

Air filter part number: _____ location found _____

Fuel filter part number: _____ location found _____

AC generator (alternator) output: _____ amps location found _____

Bore and stroke of the engine: bore _____ stroke _____ location found _____

Valve cover bolt torque specification: _____ location found _____

We Support
Education Foundation

Vehicle Safety Certification Label

Meets ASE Task: (A1 through A8-A-2) P-1 Locate and interpret vehicle and major component identification numbers

Name _____ **Date** _____ **Time on Task** _____

Make/Model/Year _____ **VIN** _____ **Evaluation: 4   3   2   1**

_____ **1.** Describe the location of the Vehicle Safety Certification Label (usually located on the driver's side pillar post).

_____

MFD BY GENERAL MOTORS OF CANADA LTD.

| GM | DATE 06/02 | GVWR 2071 KG 4565 LB | GAWR FRT 1115 KG 2458 LB | GAWR RR 956 KG 2107 LB |

THIS VEHICLE CONFORMS TO ALL APPLICABLE U.S. FEDERAL MOTOR VEHICLE SAFETY, BUMPER, AND THEFT PREVENTION STANDARDS IN EFFECT ON THE DATE OF MANUFACTURE SHOWN ABOVE.

2G1WF52E839104270   TYPE: PASS CAR

_____ **2.** What is the month and year the vehicle was manufactured?

Month = _____

Year = _____

_____ **3.** What is the gross vehicle weight rating (GVWR)?

_____

_____ **4.** What is the gross axle weight rating (GAWR)?

_____

_____ **5.** Is the exact date of manufacture listed on the label?

____ Yes   Month = _____   Day = _____   Year = _____

____ No

We Support

Work Order

Meets ASE Task: (A1-A-1) P-1 Complete work order and complete necessary customer and vehicle information.

Name _____ **Date** _____ **Time on Task** _____

Make/Model/Year _____ **VIN** _____ **Evaluation: 4   3   2   1**

_____ **1.** List the items about the **vehicle** that should be included on the work order (also called a repair order - R.O).

       a. _____   e. _____

       b. _____   f. _____

       c. _____   g. _____

       d. _____   h. _____

_____ **2.** List the information about the **driver/owner** that should be included on the work order.

       a. _____

       b. _____

       c. _____

       d. _____

_____ **3.** List the three Cs (concern, cause, and correction) that the service technician should write on the work order for a repair that includes a diagnosis of the problem (concern), the replacement of a part, and the verification of the repair.

       a. _____

       b. _____

       c. _____

Vehicle Emission Control Information

Meets ASE Task: (A1 through A8-A-2) P-1 Research vehicle and service information.

Name _____ **Date** _____ **Time on Task** _____

Make/Model/Year _____ **VIN** _____ **Evaluation: 4   3   2   1**

_____ **1.** Locate the vehicle emission control information (VECI) sticker and describe its

location: _____

```
TOYOTA   VEHICLE EMISSION CONTROL INFORMATION
         TOYOTA MOTOR CORPORATION
TEST GROUP : 7TYXV01.5HC1          EVAP. FAMILY : 7TYXR0030A42
SFI, A/FS, WU-TWC, HO2S, TWC       1.5 LITER
ENGINE TUNE-UP SPECIFICATIONS FOR ALL ALTITUDES
VALVE CLEARANCE  INTAKE    0.17-0.23  mm (0.007-0.009 in.)
(ENGINE AT COLD) EXHAUST   0.27-0.33  mm (0.011-0.013 in.)
NO OTHER ADJUSTMENTS NEEDED.
THIS VEHICLE CONFORMS TO U.S. EPA REGULATIONS APPLICABLE
TO GASOLINE-FUELED 2007 MODEL YEAR NEW TIER 2 BIN 3
MOTOR VEHICLES AND TO CALIFORNIA REGULATIONS APPLICABLE TO
2007 MODEL YEAR NEW LEV-II SULEV PASSENGER CARS.
                                        CATALYST
                                  [OBD II CERTIFIED]
21160            1NZ-FXE   USA&CANADA        8V
```

_____ **2.** List what service information is included on the sticker: _____

_____

_____

_____ **3.** List emission control devices on the vehicle: _____

_____

_____

_____ **4.** What is the U.S. Federal emission rating of the vehicle? _____

_____ **5.** What is the California emission rating of the vehicle? _____

We Support
ASE | Education Foundation

Shop Safety Checklist

Meets ASE Task: (Not specified by ASE)

Name _____ **Date** _____ **Time on Task** _____

Make/Model/Year _____ **VIN** _____ **Evaluation: 4   3   2   1**

_____ 1. Walk through the shop(s) area of the school or a local shop or dealership and check for the following items:

      a. Shields on bench or pedestal grinders   Yes___ No___ NA___

      b. Exhaust hoses in good repair   Yes___ No___ NA___

      c. Fire extinguisher installed and charged   Yes___ No___ NA___

      d. First aid kit visible and fully stocked   Yes___ No___ NA___

      e. Fire blanket visible and useable   Yes___ No___ NA___

      f. Eye wash station visible and usable   Yes___ No___ NA___

_____ 2. List anything that should be included in a safe shop that was not present.

_____

_____

_____ 3. What items of personal protective equipment were being worn by service technicians?

      a. Safety glasses/face shield   Yes___ No___ NA___

      b. Protective gloves   Yes___ No___ NA___

      c. Hearing protection   Yes___ No___ NA___

      d. Bump cap   Yes___ No___ NA___

Pearson

Fire Extinguisher

Meets ASE Task: (Not specified by ASE)

Name _____ **Date** _____ **Time on Task** _____

Make/Model/Year _____ **VIN** _____ **Evaluation: 4   3   2   1**

_____ 1. Describe the location of the fire extinguishers in your building or shop and note the last inspection dates.

Type of Extinguisher	Location	Inspection Date
_____	_____	_____
_____	_____	_____
_____	_____	_____
_____	_____	_____

_____ 2. Do any of the fire extinguishers need to be charged?

_____ Yes (which ones) _____

_____ No

_____ 3. Where can the fire extinguishers be recharged? List the name and telephone number of the company. _____ _____

_____ 4. What is the cost to recharge the fire extinguishers?

a. Water =   _____

b. CO_2 =   _____

c. Dry chemical =   _____

Hand Tool Identification

Meets ASE Task: (Not specified by ASE)

Name _____ **Date** _____ **Time on Task** _____

Make/Model/Year _____ **VIN** _____ **Evaluation:** 4   3   2   1

_____ 1. List the sizes of **wrenches** you have in
your tool box. _____

_____

_____

What sizes are missing or will need to be

purchased? _____

_____

_____ 2. List the sizes of the **1/4 inch drive sockets** you have in your tool box. _____

_____

What sizes are missing or will need to be purchased? _____

_____

_____ 3. List the sizes of the **3/8 inch drive sockets** you have in your tool box. _____

_____

What sizes are missing or will need to be purchased? _____

_____

_____ 4. List the sizes of the **1/2 inch drive sockets** you have in your tool box. _____

_____

What sizes are missing or will need to be purchased? _____

_____

_____ 5. List the **other tools** you have in your tool box including hammers, screwdrivers,

pliers, and other items. _____

_____

List additional tools that you wish to add to your tool box. _____

_____

Pearson

11

We Support ASE | Education Foundation

Power and Shop Equipment Safety Survey

Meets ASE Task: (Not specified by ASE)

Name _____ **Date** _____ **Time on Task** _____

Make/Model/Year _____ **VIN** _____ **Evaluation: 4 3 2 1**

_____ 1. Check the power and shop equipment in the shop, at a local shop, or dealer. Where was this survey taken? _____

_____ 2. List all shop equipment, such as hoists, floor jacks, and cranes, and not whether they are equipped with all needed safety devices.

Shop Equipment	Safety devices? If not, list:
_____	Yes__ No__ (describe) _____
_____	Yes__ No__ (describe) _____
_____	Yes__ No__ (describe) _____
_____	Yes__ No__ (describe) _____
_____	Yes__ No__ (describe) _____
_____	Yes__ No__ (describe) _____

_____ 3. List all power equipment, such as trouble lights, grinders, etc. and note whether they are equipped with all needed safety devices.

Power Equipment	Safety devices? If not, list:
_____	Yes__ No__ (describe) _____
_____	Yes__ No__ (describe) _____
_____	Yes__ No__ (describe) _____
_____	Yes__ No__ (describe) _____
_____	Yes__ No__ (describe) _____

We Support
Education Foundation

Oxy-Acetylene Torch Usage

Meets ASE Task: (Not specified by ASE)

Name _____ **Date** _____ **Time on Task** _____

Make/Model/Year _____ **VIN** _____ **Evaluation: 4   3   2   1**

Caution: Proper operation of an oxy-acetylene torch requires proper instruction and willingness to follow all safety precautions.

Instructor check that proper instruction has been given on the safe use of the oxy-acetylene torch.

_____

_____ **1.** Setup the torch and pressures to heat metal.

Oxygen pressure set to _____

Acetylene pressure set to _____

Instructor's OK _____

_____ **2.** Setup torch to cut metal.

Oxygen pressure set to _____

Acetylene pressure set to _____

Instructor's OK _____

Vehicle Hoisting

Meets ASE Task: (Not specified by ASE)

Name _____ Date _____ Time on Task _____

Make/Model/Year _____ VIN _____ Evaluation: 4 3 2 1

_____ 1. Drive the vehicle into position to be hoisted (lifted) being certain to center the vehicle in the stall.

_____ 2. Pull the vehicle forward until the front tire rests on the tire pad (if equipped).

_____ 3. Place the gear selector into the park position (if the vehicle has an automatic transmission/transaxle) or in neutral (if the vehicle has a manual transmission/transaxle) and firmly apply the parking brake.

_____ 4. Lower the driver's side window before exiting the vehicle. (This step helps prevent keys from being accidentally being locked in the vehicle.)

_____ 5. Position the arms and hoist pads under the frame or pinch-weld seams of the body.

Hoisting the Vehicle

_____ 6. Slowly raise the vehicle about one foot (30 cm) off the ground and check the stability of the vehicle by attempting to move the vehicle on the lift.

_____ 7. If the vehicle is stable and all pads are properly positioned under the vehicle, continue hoisting the vehicle to the height needed.

NOTE: Best working conditions are at chest or elbow level.

_____ 8. Be sure the safety latches have engaged before working under the vehicle.

Lowering the Vehicle

_____ 9. To lower the vehicle, raise the hoist slightly, then release the safety latches.

_____ 10. Lower the vehicle using the proper operating and safety release levers.

CAUTION: Do not look away while lowering the vehicle. One side of the vehicle could become stuck or something (or someone) could get under the vehicle.

_____ 11. After lowering the hoist arms all the way to the floor, move the arms so that they will not be hit when the vehicle is driven out of the stall.

We Support

Safety Data Sheet (SDS)

Meets ASE Task: (Not specified by ASE)

Name _____ **Date** _____ **Time on Task** _____

Make/Model/Year _____ **VIN** _____ **Evaluation: 4   3   2   1**

_____ **1.** Locate the SDS sheets and describe their location _____

_____

_____ **2.** Select three commonly used chemicals or solvents. Record the following information
from the SDS:

- **Product name** _____

     Chemical name(s) _____

     Does the chemical contain "chlor" or "fluor" which may indicate hazardous

     materials?   **Yes** _____   **No** _____

     flash point = _____ (hopefully above 140° F)

     pH _____ (7 = neutral, higher than 7 = caustic (base), lower than 7 = acid)

- **Product name** _____

     Chemical name(s) _____

     Does the chemical contain "chlor" or "fluor" which may indicate hazardous

     materials?   **Yes** _____   **No** _____

     flash point = _____ (hopefully above 140° F)

     pH _____ (7 = neutral, higher than 7 = caustic (base), lower than 7 = acid)

- **Product name** _____

     Chemical name(s) _____

     Does the chemical contain "chlor" or "fluor" which may indicate hazardous

     materials?   **Yes** _____   **No** _____

     flash point = _____ (hopefully above 140° F)

     pH _____ (7 = neutral, higher than 7 = caustic (base), lower than 7 = acid)

Pearson

Identify and Interpret Brake Concerns

Meets ASE Task: (A5-A-1) P-1 Identify and interpret brake system concern and determine needed action.

Name _____ Date _____ Time on Task _____

Make/Model/Year _____ VIN _____ Evaluation: 4 3 2 1

_____ 1. Verify the customer's concern regarding brake system performance and identify areas of concern (check all that apply).

_____ Red brake warning light on
_____ Amber ABS warning light on
_____ Noise during braking
_____ Noise while driving
_____ Pulling during braking
_____ Hard brake pedal
_____ Low brake pedal
_____ Spongy brake pedal
_____ Pulsating brake pedal
_____ Steering wheel vibration
_____ Other (describe) _____

_____ 2. Perform a thorough visual inspection and note any possible problems.

_____ Tires (all the same brand, size, inflation, and condition)
_____ OK _____ NOT OK **Describe** _____

_____ Brake fluid (check all that apply)
_____ OK _____ **Dirty** _____ **Low**

_____ Front disc brakes
_____ OK _____ NOT OK **Describe** _____

_____ Rear brakes
_____ OK _____ NOT OK **Describe** _____

_____ Hydraulic lines, parts, and fittings
_____ OK _____ NOT OK **Describe** _____

_____ 3. Based on the symptoms and the inspection, what service and/or parts will be needed to restore like-new braking system performance?

_____

_____

Brake System Component Identification

Meets ASE Task: (A5-A-2) P-1 Research applicable vehicle and service information, such as brake system operation, etc.

Name _____ **Date** _____ **Time on Task** _____

Make/Model/Year _____ **VIN** _____ **Evaluation: 4 3 2 1**

_____ **1.** Front disc brake design type (check all that apply):

    ___ A. Single piston caliper
    ___ B. Piston caliper
    ___ C. Four or six piston caliper
    ___ D. Fixed-type caliper design
    ___ E. Floating- or sliding-type caliper design

_____ **2.** Front rotor:

    ___ A. Vented
    ___ B. Solid

_____ **3.** Rear brakes (check all that apply):

    ___ A. Drum brakes
    ___ B. Disc brakes with integral parking brake
    ___ C. Disc brake with auxiliary parking drum brake
    ___ D. Other (describe) _____

_____ **4.** Type of parking brake application:

    ___ Hand operated
    ___ Foot operated
    ___ Electric

_____ **5.** Type of parking brakes (check which):

    ___ Drum brake
    ___ Part of rear disc brake
    ___ Separate drum brake along with rear disc brake
    ___ Other (describe) _____

Pearson

Brake System Principles

Meets ASE Task: (Task not specified by ASE)

Name _____ **Date** _____ **Time on Task** _____

Make/Model/Year _____ **VIN** _____ **Evaluation: 4   3   2   1**

The energy required to slow and/or stop a vehicle depends on two major factors:

- Weight of the vehicle
- Speed of the Vehicle

GM — MFD BY GENERAL MOTORS CORP

| DATE 07/03 | GVWR 2089 KG 4606 LB | GAWR FRT 997 KG 2198 LB | GAWR RR 1092 KG 2408 LB |

THIS VEHICLE CONFORMS TO ALL APPLICABLE U.S. FEDERAL MOTOR VEHICLE SAFETY, BUMPER, AND THEFT PREVENTION STANDARDS IN EFFECT ON THE DATE OF MANUFACTURE SHOWN ABOVE.

1G6DM577940107143   TYPE: PASS CAR

_____ 1. Check service information and determine the weight of the vehicle.

Weight = _____

_____ 2. Add the number of possible passengers (one for each location equipped with seat belts times 150 pounds each):

Number of passengers = _____ × 150 pounds = _____

_____ 3. Add possible luggage or cargo (see tire pressure decal) weight:

Luggage or cargo = _____

_____ 4. Total vehicle weight = _____

_____ 5. Using the formula, determine the kinetic energy at the following speeds:

$$\frac{weight \times speed^2}{29.9} = kinetic\ energy$$

30 mph = _____

60 mph = _____

Pearson

We Support
ASE | Education Foundation

Brake Friction Material Identification

Meets ASE Task: (Task not specified by ASE)

Name ______________________ **Date** __________ **Time on Task** __________

Make/Model/Year _______________ **VIN** _______________ **Evaluation: 4 3 2 1**

_____ **1.** Check service information for the specified brake pad edge code.________________
____

_____ **2.** What is the specified disc brake pad material (if specified)? Check any that apply.
___ None specified
___ Ceramic
___ Semi-met
___ Non-organic synthetic
___ Other (specify) ______________________________________

_____ **3.** Leaf Mark – What leaf mark is displayed on the replacement disc brake package?
___ None
___ One leaf, contains 5% or more copper
___ Two leafs – contains between 0.5% and 5% copper
___ Three leafs – contains less than 0.5% copper

We Support
ASE | Education Foundation

Hydraulic Pressure Analysis

Meets ASE Task: (A5-B-1) P-1 Diagnose pressure concerns in the brake system using hydraulic principles.

Name _____ **Date** _____ **Time on Task** _____

Make/Model/Year _____ **VIN** _____ **Evaluation: 4 3 2 1**

_____ **1.** Remove the disc brake calipers and install a force gauge between the caliper piston and the caliper housing.

_____ **2.** Depress the brake pedal and observe the force readings.

Left side = _____ pounds   Right side = _____ pounds

The readings should be the same. **OK** _____   **NOT OK** _____

_____ **3.** List possible causes that could prevent the force reading to be different from one side to the other.

A. _____

B. _____

C. _____

_____ **4.** Based on the test results, what is the needed action?

_____

_____

Pearson

We Support

Education Foundation

Brake Pedal Height

Meets ASE Task: (A5-B-2) P-1 Measure brake pedal height; determine needed action.

Name _____ Date _____ Time on Task _____

Make/Model/Year _____ VIN _____ Evaluation: 4 3 2 1

_____ **1.** State the vehicle manufacturer's specified brake height testing procedure:

_____

_____

_____

_____ **2.** Measure the brake pedal height from the bottom
of the steering wheel or floor to the brake pedal.

_____ = inch (cm)

_____ **3.** Depress the brake pedal until the brakes are
applied and measure the brake pedal height.

_____ = inch (cm)

_____ **4.** Subtract the second reading from the first
reading. This is the brake pedal travel.

_____ = brake pedal travel (should be a maximum of 2.0 to 2.5 in.)

_____ **5.** List three items that could cause a greater than normal brake pedal travel.

A. _____

B. _____

C. _____

_____ **6.** Based on the test results, what is the needed action: _____

_____

Pearson

Master Cylinder Service

Meets ASE Task: (A5-B-3) P-1, (A5-B-4) P-1 Check master cylinder for external and internal leaks and proper operation; remove, bench bleed, and reinstall master cylinder.

_____

Name _____ Date _____ Time on Task _____

Make/Model/Year _____ VIN _____ Evaluation: 4 3 2 1

_____ 1. Check visually for signs of external brake fluid leaks.

       _____ **OK** _____ **NOT OK**

       Describe location _____

FLUID RESERVOIRS   FLUID

_____ 2. Check for internal leakage by observing the level of brake fluid in the front compared to the rear.

       A. Is the level higher in the front than the rear? _____ **Yes** _____ **No**

       B. Is the brake pedal lower than normal? _____ **Yes** _____ **No**

       If yes to both A and B above, then the master cylinder is leaking internally and must be replaced.

_____ 3. Have an assistant depress the brake pedal while watching the brake fluid in the master cylinder reservoir. The brake fluid should be seen to move as the brake pedal is being depressed if the sealing caps are OK and positioned correctly.

       Movement observed?   _____ **Yes** _____ **No**

       If brake fluid does not move and there is a braking system problem, the master cylinder or linkage adjustment is faulty.

_____ 4. Based on the test results, what is the needed action? _____

_____

Hydraulic System Fault Analysis

Meets ASE Task: (A5-B-5) P-1 Diagnose braking concerns caused by hydraulic malfunctions.

Name _____ **Date** _____ **Time on Task** _____

Make/Model/Year _____ **VIN** _____ **Evaluation: 4 3 2 1**

Poor stopping or dragging brakes or pulling can be caused by hydraulic system failure or faults.

_____ 1. Check master cylinder for proper brake fluid level and condition.

_____ 2. Verify proper operation of the base brakes.
  _____ OK
  _____ Pulls to the left during braking (see Step 3).
  _____ Pulls to the right during braking (see Step 3).
  _____ Brakes do not release fully (see Step 4).
  _____ Poor stopping (see Step 5).
  _____ Other brake system concerns (describe) _____

_____ 3. Pulling can be caused by a stuck caliper piston on the side *opposite* the direction of the pull.

  If there is a pull to the right during braking, check the left side caliper.
  OK ____ **NOT OK** ____

  If there is a pull to the left during braking, check the right side caliper.
  OK ____ **NOT OK** ____

_____ 4. Brakes that do not fully release can be caused by a fault with the flexible brake hose and/or a stuck caliper piston

  Visually check the flexible brake hose. **OK** ____ **NOT OK** ____

  Check that the caliper piston can be moved into the caliper bore easily.
  OK ____ **NOT OK** ____

_____ 5. Poor stopping can be caused by a stuck caliper or wheel cylinder piston. Check that all hydraulic pistons are free.

  LF = **OK** ____   **NOT OK** ____
  RF = **OK** ____   **NOT OK** ____
  LR = **OK** ____   **NOT OK** ____
  RR= **OK** ____   **NOT OK** ____

Pearson

Brake Control Valves

Meets ASE Task: (A5-B-5) P-1 Inspect, test, and/or replace metering (hold-off), proportioning (balance), pressure differential, and combination valves. (P-3)

Name _____ Date _____ Time on Task _____

Make/Model/Year _____ VIN _____ Evaluation: 4 3 2 1

_____ **1.** Check service information and determine what brake control valves are present on the vehicle being checked/serviced.

    ___ Metering valve (describe location) _____

    _____

    ___ Proportioning valve (describe location) _____

    _____

    ___ Pressure differential switch (describe location) _____

    _____

    ___ Combination valve (describe location) _____

    _____

_____ **2.** What is the specified testing procedures associated with the control valves that are present on the vehicle. Describe the testing procedures. _____

_____

_____

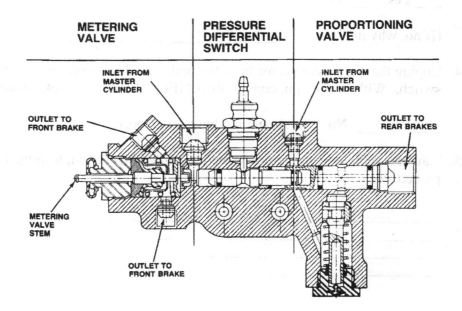

Red Brake Warning Lamp Diagnosis

Meets ASE Task: (A-5-B-10) P-3, (A5-B-11) P-2 Inspect, test and/or replace components of brake warning light system.

Name _____ **Date** _____ **Time on Task** _____

Make/Model/Year _____ **VIN** _____ **Evaluation: 4   3   2   1**

_____ **1.** Does the vehicle use a brake fluid level sensor?

   ___ Yes ___ No

   (If yes, describe the location: _____.)

_____ **2.** Does the vehicle use a pressure differential switch?

   ___ Yes ___ No

   (If yes, describe the location: _____.)

_____ **3.** With the ignition key on, engine off (KOEO), apply the parking brake. Did the red brake warning lamp light?

   ___ Yes ___ No

   (If no, why not? _____)

_____ **4.** Unplug the wiring connector from the brake fluid level sensor or pressure differential switch. With the key on, engine off (KOEO), did the red brake warning lamp light?

   ___ Yes ___ No   (It should not have come on.)

_____ **5.** State the vehicle manufacturer's recommended inspection, testing, and replacement procedures:

   _____

   _____

   _____

   _____

Brake Stop Light Switch

Meets ASE Task: (A5-F-5) P-1 Check operation of brake stop light system and determine needed action.

Name _____ **Date** _____ **Time on Task** _____

Make/Model/Year _____ **VIN** _____ **Evaluation: 4   3   2   1**

_____ 1. Check the service information for the specified testing procedures to determine the proper operation and adjustment of the brake stop light switch. _____

_____

_____

_____ 2. Check for the proper operation of the brake (stop) lights including the center high-mounted stop light (CHMSL).

   OK ____   **NOT OK** ____

   If not OK, determine the needed action needed to restore proper operation.

_____

_____

_____ 3. Describe the location of the brake switch _____

_____ 4. Describe how to adjust the brake switch (if adjustable) _____

_____

_____ 5. List the trade number of the brake light bulbs, including the center high-mounted stop light.

   Rear brake light trade number = _____

   Center high-mounted stop light trade number = _____

_____ 6. Based on the test results, what is the needed action? _____

_____

_____

Brake Hoses and Lines

Meets ASE Task: (A5-B-6) P-1, (A5-B-7) P-2, (A5-B-8) P-2 Brake hose and line inspection and replacement.

Name _____ **Date** _____ **Time on Task** _____

Make/Model/Year _____ **VIN** _____ **Evaluation: 4   3   2   1**

_____ **1.** Check service information for the specified procedure to follow when inspecting and/or replacing brake hoses and lines. Describe the recommended procedures.

_____

_____

_____ **2.** Based on the inspection of the brake lines and hoses, what is the needed action?

_____

_____

_____

_____

_____ **3.** Using the specified diameter of brake line, perform the two brake line flaring procedure.

    _____ Double flare   **Instructor's check** _____

    _____ ISO (bubble) flare   **Instructor's check** _____

_____ **4.** Bend brake line as needed.   **Instructor's check** _____

_____ **5.** List the trade number of the brake light bulbs, including the center high-mounted stop light.

Rear brake light trade number = _____

Center high-mounted stop light trade number = _____

_____ **6.** Based on the test results, what is the needed action? _____

Brake Fluid

Meets ASE Task: (A5-B-9) P-1, (A5-B-13) P-1 Brake fluid usage and test for contamination.

Name _____ **Date** _____ **Time on Task** _____

Make/Model/Year _____ **VIN** _____ **Evaluation:** 4 3 2 1

_____ 1. Check service information for the specified brake fluid and when to check for the proper level.

    A. Specified brake fluid = _____

    B. Specified brake fluid level _____ (describe the location) _____

_____ 2. Check service information for the recommended procedure to follow to determine if the brake fluid is contaminated. Describe the specified procedure:

    _____

    _____

_____ 3. Check all that apply according to service information.

    _____ Perform a visual inspection.

    _____ Place the sample in styrofoam cup and check for eating away of the cup at the top of the fluid level line.

    _____ Use a test strip.

    _____ Use a brake fluid boiling temperature tester

    _____ Other (describe) _____

We Support

Brake Bleeding

Meets ASE Task: (A5-B-12) P-1 Bleed and/or flush the brake system.

Name _____ **Date** _____ **Time on Task** _____

Make/Model/Year _____ **VIN** _____ **Evaluation:** 4 3 2 1

_____ 1. Check service information for the specified procedure to follow when bleeding and/or flushing the brake system. Describe the specified procedure.

_____

_____

_____ 2. Perform a brake bleeding/flushing procedure. **Instructor's check** _____

_____ 3. Which method(s) was used (check all that apply)?

_____ Normal (single stroke) method

_____ Pressure bleeding

_____ Vacuum bleeding

_____ Gravity bleeding

_____ Brake system was flushed

_____ 4. Was the use of a scan tool needed or suggested?

_____ Yes (What scan tool?) _____

_____ No

Wheel Bearing Diagnosis

Meets ASE Task: (A5-F-1) P-1 Diagnose wheel bearing noises, wheel shimmy, and vibration concerns; determine needed action.

Name _____ **Date** _____ **Time on Task** _____

Make/Model/Year _____ **VIN** _____ **Evaluation: 4   3   2   1**

Worn or defective wheel bearings can cause a variety of concerns including:

Noise – usually a growl or rumble that changes tone with vehicle speed.

Wheel Shimmy – Can occur if the bearings are loose or excessively worn.

Vibration – Can occur if the bearings are loose or excessively worn.

_____ 1. Check service information for the recommended test procedures to follow to diagnose possible wheel bearing noise.

_____
_____

_____ 2. Drive the vehicle and check for abnormal noise that could be caused by a defective wheel bearing.

   OK _____   **NOT OK** _____

   HINT: A defective wheel bearing often sounds like a noisy winter tire but does not change tone when the vehicle is being driven over various road surfaces.

_____ 3. Hoist the vehicle safely and check for excessive wheel bearing play and/or noise.

   OK _____   **NOT OK** _____

   Describe the faults and location: _____

_____ 4. Based on the diagnosis, what is the needed action? _____

_____

_____

We Support
Education Foundation

Wheel Bearing Service

Meets ASE Task: (A5-F-2) P-2 Remove, clean, inspect, repack, and install wheel bearings.

Name _____ **Date** _____ **Time on Task** _____

Make/Model/Year _____ **VIN** _____ **Evaluation: 4   3   2   1**

_____ **1.** Remove the wheel cover and the hub dust cap (grease cap).

_____ **2.** Remove and discard the cotter key.

_____ **3.** Remove the spindle nut, washer and outer bearing.

_____ **4.** Remove inner and outer bearing and grease seal.

_____ **5.** Thoroughly clean the bearing in solvent and denatured alcohol or brake cleaner and blow it dry with compressed air.

_____ **6.** Closely inspect the bearing for wear or damage.

_____ **7.** Show the instructor the cleaned bearing.   **Instructor's OK** _____

_____ **8.** Repack the bearing with the correct type of wheel bearing grease.

_____ **9.** Install a new grease seal using a seal installing tool.

_____ **10.** Correctly adjust the bearing preload:

　　　____ Install the spindle nut and while rotating the tire assembly, tighten (snug only, 12 to 30 lb.-ft.) with a wrench to "seat" the bearing correctly in the race.
　　　____ While still rotating the tire assembly, loosen the nut approximately 1/2 turn and then *hand tighten only*.
　　　____ Install a new cotter key (the common size is 1/8" diameter and 1.5 inches long).
　　　____ Bend the ends of the cotter key up and around the nut to prevent interference with the dust cap.

_____ **11.** Install the hub dust cap (grease cap) and wheel cover.

Wheel Bearing and Race Replacement

Meets ASE Task: (A5-F-6) P-3, (A4-D-2) P-1 Replace wheel bearing and race.

Name _____ **Date** _____ **Time on Task** _____

Make/Model/Year _____ **VIN** _____ **Evaluation: 4   3   2   1**

_____ **1.** Remove the wheel cover and the hub dust cap (grease cap).

_____ **2.** Remove and discard the cotter key.

_____ **3.** Remove the spindle nut, washer and outer bearing.

_____ **4.** Remove inner and outer bearing and grease seal.

_____ **5.** Remove the bearing race using the specified tool.

_____ **6.** Show the instructor the removed race.   **Instructor's OK** _____

_____ **7.** Install new race using the correct bearing race installation tool.

_____ **8.** Show the instructor the new race.   **Instructor's OK** _____

_____ **9.** Install a new grease seal using a seal installing tool.

_____ **10.** Pack the new bearing with the correct type of wheel bearing grease.

_____ **11.** Correctly adjust the bearing preload:

> _____ Install the spindle nut and while rotating the tire assembly, tighten (snug only, 12 to 30 lb.-ft.) with a wrench to "seat" the bearing correctly in the race.
> _____ While still rotating the tire assembly, loosen the nut approximately 1/2 turn and then *hand tighten only*.
> _____ Install a new cotter key (the common size is 1/8" diameter and 1.5 inches long).
> _____ Bend the ends of the cotter key up and around the nut to prevent interference with the dust cap.

_____ **12.** Install the hub dust cap (grease cap) and wheel cover.

Pearson

We Support
ASE | Education Foundation

Inspect and Replace Wheel Studs

Meets ASE Task: (A5-F-8) P-1 Inspect and replace wheel studs.

Name _____ **Date** _____ **Time on Task** _____

Make/Model/Year _____ **VIN** _____ **Evaluation: 4   3   2   1**

_____ **1.** Hoist the vehicle safely.

_____ **2.** Remove all four wheels.

_____ **3.** Carefully inspect the wheel studs for excessive rust or damage.

LF = OK _____   **NOT OK** _____ Describe fault _____

RF = OK _____   **NOT OK** _____ Describe fault _____

LR = OK _____   **NOT OK** _____ Describe fault _____

RR = OK _____   **NOT OK** _____ Describe fault _____

_____ **4.** Clean the threads using a stiff wire brush.

CAUTION: Many vehicle manufacturers specify that grease or oil should *not* be used on the threads of wheel studs. If a lubricant is used on the threads, the lug nuts could loosen during vehicle operation, which could cause a wheel to fall off resulting in a collision and possible personal injury.

_____ **5.** Worn or damaged studs should be replaced. Check the service information for the specified procedure for replacing wheel studs on the vehicle being serviced.

_____

_____ **6.** Which stud(s) were replaced? _____

We Support
ASE | Education Foundation

Pearson

Sealed Wheel Bearing Replacement

Meets ASE Task: (A5-F-7) P-1, (A3-D-3) P-1 Remove and install sealed wheel bearing assembly.

Name _____ Date _____ Time on Task _____

Make/Model/Year _____ VIN _____ Evaluation: 4 3 2 1

_____ 1. Check service information for the specified replacement procedure for the vehicle being serviced. _____

_____

_____ 2. Loosen (do not remove) the drive axle shaft nut.

_____ 3. Hoist the vehicle safely to a good working height (about chest high).

_____ 4. Remove the front wheel.

_____ 5. Use a steel drift between the caliper and the rotor cooling vent hole to hold the rotor from rotating.

_____ 6. Remove the drive axle shaft hub nut.

_____ 7. Remove the front disc brake caliper.

_____ 8. Remove the rotor, the hub, and splash shield retaining bolts.

_____ 9. Mark the location of the hub and make certain the hub is loose on the steering knuckle.

_____ 10. Install the hub puller and remove the bearing and hub assembly.

_____ 11. Clean and lubricate hub bearing surface.

_____ 12. Reinstall the hub and bearing using the drive axle shaft nut. (Do not torque to the final setting, just until the hub is seated.)

_____ 13. Reinstall the rotor, caliper, and wheel.

_____ 14. Lower the vehicle and tighten the drive axle shaft nut to the final specification.
Specification = _____ (usually about 200 lb.-ft.)

We Support

Education Foundation

Drum Brake Identification

Meets ASE Task: (A5-A-2) P-1 Research applicable vehicle and service information, such as brake system operation, vehicle service history, service precautions and TSBs.

Name _____ **Date** _____ **Time on Task** _____

Make/Model/Year _____ **VIN** _____ **Evaluation: 4   3   2   1**

_____ 1. Check service information and determine the following information regarding the drum brake design and features for the vehicle (check all that apply):

____ Dual servo
____ Leading trailing
____ Clip-on wheel cylinder
____ Bolted on wheel cylinder
____ Cast iron brake drum
____ Aluminum brake drum
____ Single U-spring design
____ Clip-type holddown
____ Coil-spring holddown
____ Cable-operated self adjust
____ Other (describe) _____
_____
_____

_____ 2. What is the brake drum diameter?

_____

_____ 3. What is the minimum allowable lining thickness?

_____

_____ 4. What is the maximum allowable brake drum diameter?

_____

Drum Brake Problem Diagnosis

Meets ASE Task: (A5-C-1) P-1 Diagnose drum brake concerns; determine needed action.

Name _____ **Date** _____ **Time on Task** _____

Make/Model/Year _____ **VIN** _____ **Evaluation: 4   3   2   1**

_____ **1.** Verify drum brake problem concerns.

  _____ Noise (describe) _____

  _____ Poor stopping

  _____ Pulling (toward which side?) _____

  _____ Grabbing (when?) _____

  _____ Dragging

  _____ Brake pedal pulsation

_____ **2.** Hoist the vehicle safely.

_____ **3.** Wet the brake drum or install a
vacuum enclosure to provide
protection against possible asbestos
dust.

_____ **4.** Remove the brake drums.

_____ **5.** Describe the condition of the drum brake parts:

  _____ Brake drum _____

  _____ Lining _____

  _____ Springs _____

  _____ Self-adjuster _____

  _____ Backing plate _____

_____ **6.** Based on the diagnosis, what is the needed action?

_____

_____

Drum Brake Service

Meets ASE Task: (A5-C-4) P-1, (A5-C-5) P-2, (A5-C-6) P-1 Check and replace drum brake assembly.

Name _____ **Date** _____ **Time on Task** _____

Make/Model/Year _____ **VIN** _____ **Evaluation:** 4 3 2 1

_____ **1.** Check service information for the exact procedures to follow when inspecting and replacing drum brake shoes and related hardware. Describe the recommended procedures.

_____

_____

_____ **2.** Remove, clean, and inspect the brake shoes and springs. Lubricate the backing plate.

Instructor's check _____

_____ **3.** Inspect and install the wheel cylinders. **Instructor's check** _____

_____ **4.** Assemble the drum brake assemblies and adjust the parking brake and the brake drums.

Instructor's check _____

Install Wheel and Torque Lug Nuts

Meets ASE Task: (A5-A-4) P-1 Install wheel and torque lug nuts and make final checks and adjustments.

Name _____ **Date** _____ **Time on Task** _____

Make/Model/Year _____ **VIN** _____ **Evaluation:** 4   3   2   1

_____ 1. Check service information and determine the vehicle manufacturer's specified lug nut torque specification.

   _____ (usually between 80 and 100 lb-ft)

_____ 2. Use a hand-operated wire brush on the wheel studs to ensure clean and dry threads and check for damage.

   OK _____   **NOT OK** _____   Describe fault: _____

_____ 3. Verify that the lug nuts are OK and free of defects.

_____ 4. Install the wheel over the studs and start all lug nuts (or bolts) by hand.

_____ 5. Tighten the lug nuts a little at a time in a star pattern using an air impact wrench equipped with the proper torque limiting adapter or a torque wrench.

   _____ Used a torque wrench

   _____ Used an air impact with a torque limiting adapter (torque stick)

_____ 6. Tighten the lug nuts to final torque in a star pattern.

NOTE: "Tighten one, skip one, tighten one" is the usual method if four or five lug nuts are used.

Disc Brake Identification

Meets ASE Task: (A5-A-2) P-1 Research applicable vehicle and service information, such as brake system operation, vehicle service history, service precautions, and TSBs.

Name _____ **Date** _____ **Time on Task** _____

Make/Model/Year _____ **VIN** _____ **Evaluation:** 4 3 2 1

_____ **1.** Check service information and/or check the vehicle to determine the following information:

    A. Type of brake system -   ___ Disc front brakes/drum rear brakes
                                        ___ Disc front brakes/disc rear brakes

    B. Type of disc brake caliper (check all that apply) –

         ___ Floating
         ___ Sliding
         ___ Fixed
            ___ Single piston
         ___ Two pistons
         ___ Four or six pistons

    C. Type of rotors (check all that apply)

         ___ Vented front
         ___ Vented rear
         ___ Solid front
         ___ Solid rear

    D. Location of caliper (forward or rearward) –

         Front calipers = _____
         Rear calipers = _____

    E. What sensor or switch is used to turn on the red brake warning light in the event of hydraulic failure?

         ___ Brake fluid level sensor
         ___ Pressure differential switch

Pearson

We Support

ASE | Education Foundation

Brake System Road Test

Meets ASE Task: (A5-A-3) P-1 Describe the procedure for performing a road test to check brake system operation.

Name _____ **Date** _____ **Time on Task** _____

Make/Model/Year _____ **VIN** _____ **Evaluation: 4   3   2   1**

_____ **1.** Check service information for the specified procedure to follow when performing a test drive to check for a brake system fault. Describe the specified procedure.

_____

_____

_____

_____

_____

_____ **2.** Check all that are specified.

___ Check the brake fluid level before driving

___ Check the brake pedal height

___ Perform a visual inspection of wheels/tires

___ Other (Specify) _____

_____

CAUTION: Most experts state that the vehicle should not be road tested if the red brake warning light is on. Always follow the vehicle manufacturer's recommended procedures.

Pearson

We Support

ASE | Education Foundation

Disc Brake Diagnosis and Service

Meets ASE Task: (A5-D-1) P-1, (A5-D-2) P-1, (A5-D-3) P-1, (A5-D-4) P-1, (A5-D-5) P-3
Disc brake caliper and related component inspection and service.

Name _____ **Date** _____ **Time on Task** _____

Make/Model/Year _____ **VIN** _____ **Evaluation:** 4 3 2 1

_____ **1.** Check service information for the specified procedure to follow when diagnosing and servicing disc brakes. Describe the recommended procedures.

_____

_____

_____ **2.** Perform a thorough inspection of the disc brake system, including the condition of the following:

    A. Caliper (leaks or damage)   ___ OK ___ NOT OK

    B. Caliper mounts   ___ OK ___ NOT OK

    C. Brake pads   ___ OK ___ NOT OK

_____ **3.** Based on the inspection, what is the needed action? _____

_____

_____ **4.** Disassemble, clean, and overhaul the disc brake calipers. **Instructor's check** _____

_____ **5.** Reassemble the disc brake assembly, seat the pads, bleed the brakes as needed.

Instructor's check _____

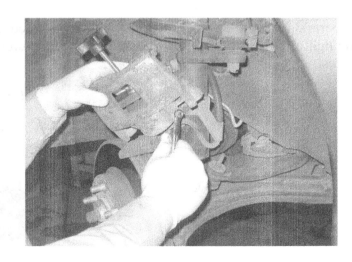

We Support
ASE | Education Foundation

Pearson

Brake Pad Wear Indicator System

Meets ASE Task: (A5-D-11) P-1 Check brake pad wear indicator system operation; determine needed action.

Name _____ **Date** _____ **Time on Task** _____

Make/Model/Year _____ **VIN** _____ **Evaluation:** 4 3 2 1

_____ **1.** Check service information for the specified procedure to follow when checking the brake pad wear indicator system. Describe specified instructions: _____

_____

_____

_____ **2.** What type of brake pad wear indicates that the system was tested? (check all that apply)

_____ **Wear sensor on pads** (makes noise when pads are worn)

_____ **Dash warning lamp** (triggered by the sensor in the brake)

_____ **Slits cut in the disc brake pads** that indicate minimum allowable thickness

_____ **3.** Based on the inspection of the brake pad wear indicator system, what is the needed action?

_____

Pearson

Brake Pad Burnishing-In Procedure

Meets ASE Task: (A5-D-12) P-1 Describe the importance of performing burnish/bedding-in replacement brake pad procedure.

Name _____ **Date** _____ **Time on Task** _____

Make/Model/Year _____ **VIN** _____ **Evaluation: 4   3   2   1**

_____ **1.** Check service information for the specified procedure to follow to burnish (bed-in) new replacement brake pads. Describe the specified procedure._____

_____

_____

_____

_____ **2.** Describe why it is important to perform the burnishing-in procedure? _____

_____

_____

_____

Pearson

We Support

ASE | **Education Foundation**

Rear Disc Parking Brake Adjustment

Meets ASE Task: (A5-D-10) P-2 Adjust calipers with integrated parking brake.

Name _____ **Date** _____ **Time on Task** _____

Make/Model/Year _____ **VIN** _____ **Evaluation: 4 3 2 1**

Many vehicles equipped with rear disc brakes use a mechanical activated parking brake that is integral with the caliper. Most are designed to be self-adjusting by adjusting when excessive brake pad-to-rotor clearance occurs.

_____ 1. Check the service information for the specified rear disc brake parking brake adjustment procedure.

_____

_____ 2. Check the number of "clicks" of the parking brake.

_____ Number of clicks (should be between 3 and 9)

OK _____ **NOT OK** _____

If over 10 clicks is needed to set the parking brake, the rear disc brake caliper needs adjustment.

_____ 3. Hoist the vehicle safely and remove both rear wheels.

_____ 4. Carefully inspect the rear disc brakes for damage and measure the pads for excessive wear.

¼" DRILL
BIT OR DOWEL

OK _____ **NOT OK** _____

Replace the pads if worn to the minimum allowable thickness.

_____ 5. If the disc brake pads are serviceable, operate the parking brake lever using the appropriate size wrench on the actuating arm retaining bolt/nut while lightly tapping on the caliper using a dead blow plastic hammer. The adjusting mechanism should cause the piston to be repositioned with the correct pad to rotor clearance.

OK _____ **NOT OK** _____

If the proper clearance is not achieved, replacement of the calipers is required.

Parking Brake Adjustment

Meets ASE Task: (A5-F-3) P-1 Check parking brake cables and components for wear and clean or replace as needed.

Name _____ **Date** _____ **Time on Task** _____

Make/Model/Year _____ **VIN** _____ **Evaluation: 4   3   2   1**

_____ **1.** Check the service information for the specified parking brake adjustment for the

vehicle being serviced. _____

_____ **2.** Apply the parking brake and count the number of "clicks."
_____ less than 4 "clicks"
_____ 5 - 10 "clicks"
_____ over 10 "clicks"

NOTE: If there are less than 4 "clicks" or more than 10 "clicks", adjustment of the parking brake may be needed.

_____ **3.** Place the gear selector in neutral and release the parking brake.
_____ **4.** Hoist the vehicle safely.
_____ **5.** Try rotating the rear wheels (front wheels on some Subaru vehicles).
_____ rotates freely

_____ does not rotate

NOTE: If the rear wheels do not rotate, try loosening the parking brake cable.

_____ **6.** If the rear wheels rotate freely and the parking brake requires more than 10 "clicks," remove the rear brakes for inspection.

NOTE: The parking brake should only be adjusted after checking and adjusting the rear brakes.

_____ **7.** Clean and adjust the rear brakes.
_____ **8.** Reassemble the rear brakes and apply the parking brake 3 - 4 "clicks."
_____ **9.** If the rear wheels can be rotated, adjust the parking brake adjuster until the rear wheel brakes are just touching the brake drums.
_____ **10.** Apply the parking brake and again count the

"clicks." Most vehicle manufacturers recommend
that the parking brake should hold with 6 to 18

"clicks." Readjust the parking brake as needed.

Pearson

We Support
ASE | Education Foundation

Parking Brake Operation

Meets ASE Task: (A5-F-4) P-1 Check parking brake operation; determine needed action.

Name _____ **Date** _____ **Time on Task** _____

Make/Model/Year _____ **VIN** _____ **Evaluation: 4   3   2   1**

_____ **1.** Check service information for the specified procedure to follow when checking the parking brake for proper operation.

_____

_____

_____

_____ **2.** Identify the type of parking brake.

_____ Foot operated

_____ Hand operated

_____ Push button

_____ **3.** Most vehicle manufacturers specify that the parking brake be applied and that the number of "clicks" required should be from 3 to 10. Apply the parking brake.

_____ **OK** (within the specified number of clicks)

_____ **NOT OK** (describe) _____

_____

_____ **4.** Based on the check of the parking brake, what is the needed action?

_____

_____

Brake Drum Service

Meets ASE Task: (A5-C-2) P-1, (A5-C-3) P-1 Inspect, measure, and machine brake drums.

Name _____ **Date** _____ **Time on Task** _____

Make/Model/Year _____ **VIN** _____ **Evaluation: 4 3 2 1**

_____ **1.** Check service information for the exact specifications and procedures to follow when inspecting, measuring, and machining brake drums. Describe specified procedures.

_____

_____

_____ **2.** Measure the drum and compare to factory specifications:

Factory specification = _____

Measured drum inside diameter = _____

____ OK   ____ NOT OK

_____ **3.** Machine the brake drum.   **Instructor's check** _____

_____ **4.** What is the measurement of the drum after machining?

_____

Brake Rotor Service

Meets ASE Task: (A5-D-6) P-1, (A5-D-7) P-1, (A5-D-8) P-1, (A5-D-9) P-1 Inspect, measure, and machine a disc brake rotor.

Name _____ **Date** _____ **Time on Task** _____

Make/Model/Year _____ **VIN** _____ **Evaluation: 4   3   2   1**

_____ 1. Check service information for the exact specifications and procedures to follow when inspecting, measuring, and machining brake rotors. Describe specified procedures.

_____

_____

_____ 2. Measure the rotors and compare to factory specifications:

Factory specification = _____

Measured rotor inside diameter = _____

____ OK   ____ NOT OK

_____ 3. Machine the brake rotor using an on-vehicle lathe.

Instructor's check _____

_____ 4. What is the measurement of the rotor after machining?

_____

Pearson

Vacuum Power Brake Booster Test

Meets ASE Task: (A5-E-1) P-2 Test pedal free travel; check power assist operation.

Name _____ **Date** _____ **Time on Task** _____

Make/Model/Year _____ **VIN** _____ **Evaluation: 4   3   2   1**

_____ 1. Check the service information for the specified procedure for testing a vacuum power brake booster for the vehicle being serviced.

_____

_____ 2. With the engine off, depress the brake pedal several times until the brake pedal feels hard (firm).

_____ 3. The brake pedal should not fall to the floor of the vehicle.

OK _____   **NOT OK** _____

NOTE: If the brake pedal travels to the floor of the vehicle, carefully inspect the hydraulic brake system for a fault. Service or repair the hydraulic brake problem before continuing with this test.

_____ 4. With your foot still firmly depressing the brake pedal, start the engine. The brake pedal should go down.
OK _____   **NOT OK** _____

_____ 5. If the brake pedal did not go down when the engine was started, visually check the following:

_____ Minimum of 15 in. Hg of vacuum to the vacuum booster from the engine manifold or auxiliary vacuum pump

_____ Proper operation of the one-way check valve

_____ Unrestricted charcoal filter between the booster and the intake manifold (if equipped)

_____ Inspect for vacuum leaks

OK _____   **NOT OK** _____

Pearson

Vacuum Supply/Manifold or Auxiliary Pump

Meets ASE Task: (A5-E-2) P-1 Check vacuum supply to vacuum-type power booster.

Name _____ **Date** _____ **Time on Task** _____

Make/Model/Year _____ **VIN** _____ **Evaluation: 4   3   2   1**

_____ 1. Check service information for the recommended procedures and specifications for checking vacuum supply to power booster.

_____

_____

_____

_____ 2. Is the vehicle equipped with an auxiliary vacuum pump?   ____ Yes   ____ No

_____ 3. Most vehicle manufacturers specify that a vacuum "T" be installed in the vacuum line between the intake manifold and/or auxiliary pump and the vacuum power brake booster assembly. Most manufacturers specify a minimum of 15 in. Hg. of vacuum be measured.

Actual vacuum measured at the power brake booster = _____

____ OK   ____ NOT OK

Pearson

We Support

ASE | Education Foundation

Vacuum-Type Power Booster

Meets ASE Task: (A5-E-3) P-1 Inspect vacuum-type power booster unit for vacuum leaks; inspect the check valve for proper operation; determine needed action.

Name _____ **Date** _____ **Time on Task** _____

Make/Model/Year _____ **VIN** _____ **Evaluation: 4 3 2 1**

_____ **1.** Check service information for the recommended procedures to follow to determine if a vacuum-type power brake booster has a vacuum leak.

_____

_____

_____

_____ **2.** Most vacuum-type power boosters should be capable of supplying 3 or more assisted stops with the engine off. How many were found? _____

_____ **3.** Most vehicle manufacturers specify checking for leaks both around the outside (under the hood), as well as in the valve area under the instrument panel.

Under hood:

____ OK   ____ NOT OK

Valve area:

____ OK   ____ NOT OK

_____ **4.** Based on the test results, what is the needed action? _____

_____

Pearson

Hydro-Boost Test

Meets ASE Task: (A5-E-4) P-3 Inspect and test hydro-boost system for leaks and proper operation.

Name _____ Date _____ Time on Task _____

Make/Model/Year _____ VIN _____ Evaluation: 4 3 2 1

_____ 1. Check the service information for the specified Hydro-Boost testing procedure for the vehicle being serviced.

_____

_____ 2. Start the testing of a Hydro-boost power brake assist system by carefully inspecting the following components:

    Power steering fluid level   OK _____   NOT OK _____
    Power steering pressure hoses for leaks   OK _____   NOT OK _____
    Power steering pump drive belt   OK _____   NOT OK _____
    Master cylinder brake fluid level   OK _____   NOT OK _____
    Visually inspect the Hydro-boost assembly
    for evidence of power steering fluid leaks OK _____   NOT OK _____

_____ 3. Check the operation of the base hydraulic brakes by depressing the brake pedal several times with the engine "off" until the brake pedal feels firm. Continue to apply force to the brake pedal. The brake pedal should *not* drop.
    OK _____   NOT OK _____(master cylinder or hydraulic system fault is indicated)

_____ 4. With your foot still applying force to the brake pedal, start the engine. If the Hydro-boost system is functioning correctly, the brake pedal should drop.
    OK _____   NOT OK _____

_____ 5. To check the power steering pump for proper operation, connect a power steering pressure gauge or pressure and volume gauge between the pump and the Hydro-boost unit. Start the engine and observe the pressure and volume gauges.
    Pressure at idle = _____
    (should be less than 150 psi)
    OK _____   NOT OK _____

    Volume at idle = _____
    (should be at least 2 gallons per minute)
    OK _____   NOT OK _____

Pearson

Master Cylinder Pushrod Length

Meets ASE Task: (A5-E-5) P-3 Measure and adjust master cylinder pushrod length.

Name _____ **Date** _____ **Time on Task** _____

Make/Model/Year _____ **VIN** _____ **Evaluation: 4   3   2   1**

_____ **1.** Check service information for the specified procedures and specifications for checking and adjusting master cylinder pushrod length.

_____

_____

VACUUM BRAKE
BOOSTER

ADJUSTER

VACUUM
HOSE

PUSHROD (HOLD)

_____ **2.** Where is the measurement taken?

_____

_____ **3.** Is a "go-no go" gauge needed? If so, what is the part number? _____

_____ **4.** Describe the symptoms if the master cylinder pushrod length is not correct.

_____

_____

Pearson

Electronic Brake Control System Components

Meets ASE Task: (A5-G-1) P-1 Identify traction control/vehicle stability control system components.

Name _____ **Date** _____ **Time on Task** _____

Make/Model/Year _____ **VIN** _____ **Evaluation:**   4   3   2   1

_____ 1. Check service information to determine what components are included in the traction control/vehicle stability control system (check all that apply).

     ___ ABS electrohydraulic control unit
     ___ ABS/traction control computer (controller)
     ___ Wheel speed sensors
     ___ Steering wheel position sensor
     ___ Vehicle speed sensor
     ___ Lateral force ("G") sensor

_____ 2. Describe the location of each of the components.

_____

_____

_____

_____

_____

Pearson

We Support

ASE | Education Foundation

Electronic Brake (ABS) Component Inspection

Meets ASE Task: (A5-G-1) P-1 Identify and inspect electronic brake control system components; determine needed action.

Name _____ Date _____ Time on Task _____

Make/Model/Year _____ VIN _____ Evaluation: 4 3 2 1

_____ 1. Check service information for the identification of the electronic brake system and the exact procedure to follow during an inspection.

Type of electronic brake system = _____

Describe the specified inspection procedure: _____

_____

_____ 2. Inspect all components of the electronic brake system. (check all that apply)

_____ Master cylinder	____ OK	____ NOT OK
_____ Electrohydraulic unit	____ OK	____ NOT OK
_____ Accumulator(s)	____ OK	____ NOT OK
_____ Electronic control unit	____ OK	____ NOT OK
_____ Wheel speed sensors	____ OK	____ NOT OK

_____ Other (describe) _____

_____ 3. What tools or equipment was needed to perform the inspection and/or testing? (check all that apply)

_____ Scan tool   _____ DMM   _____ Mirror

_____ Pressure gauge   Other (describe) _____

_____ 4. Based on the inspection, what is the needed action?

_____

_____

Electronic Brake (ABS) Fault Diagnosis

Meets ASE Task: (A5-G-3) P-2, (A5-G-4) P-2 Diagnose electronic brake system faults; determine needed action.

Name _____ Date _____ Time on Task _____

Make/Model/Year _____ VIN _____ Evaluation: 4 3 2 1

_____ 1. Check service information for the recommended procedures to follow when diagnosing an electronic brake control system. Describe the specified procedure:

_____

_____

_____ 2. What tools or test equipment was specified? (check all that apply)

_____ Scan tool

_____ Pressure gauge

_____ Digital meter

_____ Other (describe) _____

_____ 3. Based on the test results, what is the needed action? _____

_____

![Dashboard warning lights showing TRAC OFF, ABS, and airbag indicator]

Depressurization of High-Pressure ABS

Meets ASE Task: (A5-G-5) P-2 Depressurize high-pressure components of the electronic brake control system.

Name _____ **Date** _____ **Time on Task** _____

Make/Model/Year _____ **VIN** _____ **Evaluation:** 4 3 2 1

Integral ABS systems combine the function of the master cylinder, power-assist booster, and antilock brake functions in one assembly. These assemblies operate at high pressure and must be depressurized before performing service work on the brake system to avoid possible personal injury.

_____ 1. Check the service information for the specified depressurization procedure for the vehicle being serviced.

_____

_____

_____ 2. Visually check the brake fluid reservoir.

Proper level?   **OK** _____   **NOT OK** _____

Brake fluid condition? Describe: _____

_____ 3. Inspect the ABS hydraulic control unit for signs of damage or leakage.

OK _____   **NOT OK** _____

_____ 4. With the ignition key off, depress the brake pedal forty (40) times. The brake pedal should be hard when depressed after the first few brake applications

OK _____   **NOT OK** _____

If the brake pedal is not hard and a power-assisted brake application is still possible, find and correct the ignition feed circuit to the hydraulic control unit before proceeding to brake system service.

Pearson

We Support
ASE | Education Foundation

Bleed ABS Hydraulic Circuits

Meets ASE Task: (A5-G-6) P-1 Bleed electronic brake control system hydraulic circuits.

Name _____ **Date** _____ **Time on Task** _____

Make/Model/Year _____ **VIN** _____ **Evaluation: 4   3   2   1**

ABS hydraulic front and rear hydraulic circuits must be bled using the exact procedure specified by the vehicle manufacturer.

_____ 1. Check the service information and state the vehicle manufacturer's specified bleeding procedure and sequence.

_____

_____

_____

_____

_____ 2. Type of brake fluid specified for use during the bleeding procedure?

_____

_____ 3. Was a scan tool required? ____ **Yes** ____ **No**   If yes, describe the procedure:

_____

_____ 4. Was a special tool or tools required? ____ **Yes** ____ **No**   If yes, describe the procedure:

_____

_____ 5. Was the bleeding procedure the same for both the front and the rear wheel brakes?

____ **Yes** ____ **No**

Pearson

ABS Wheel Speed Sensor Testing

Meets ASE Task: (A5-G-7) P-2 Test, diagnose, and service ABS wheel speed sensors.

Name _____ **Date** _____ **Time on Task** _____

Make/Model/Year _____ **VIN** _____ **Evaluation: 4   3   2   1**

A magnetic wheel speed sensor can fail in a variety of ways including: electrically shorted, open, or grounded.

_____ 1. Locate and disconnect the wheel speed sensor connector. Hoist the vehicle if needed.

_____ 2. Disconnect the wheel speed sensor (WSS) connector and connect a digital meter set to read ohms.

_____ 3. Measure the resistance at the sensor terminals.

   WSS resistance = _____

   Compare the resistance to the factory
   specifications = _____
   (usually about 1000 ohms).
   OK _____   **NOT OK** _____

_____ 4. With the meter still set to read ohms, connect one meter lead to a good clean chassis ground and the other lead to one terminal of the WSS connector. This test determines that the WSS is shorted to ground unless the meter indicates infinity (OL).

   Meter reading = _____ should be infinity (OL). **OK** _____   **NOT OK** _____

_____ 5. Set the digital meter to read AC volts.

_____ 6. Connect the leads of the meter to the terminals of the wheel speed sensor.

_____ 7. Have an assistant spin the wheel and observe the AC voltage on the meter display.

   Reading = _____ AC volts (should be over 0.1 V (100 mV)

   OK _____   **NOT OK** _____

_____ 8. Observe the wheel speed sensor using a graphing multimeter (GMM) or a digital storage oscilloscope (DSO). Draw the waveform displayed while an assistant spins the wheel.

Pearson

Modified Vehicle ABS Problem Diagnosis

Meets ASE Task: (A5-G-8) P-1 Diagnose electronic brake control system braking concerns caused by vehicle modifications (tire size, curb height, final drive ratio, etc.).

Name _____   Date _____   Time on Task _____

Make/Model/Year _____   VIN _____   Evaluation: 4   3   2   1

_____   1.   Carefully inspect the vehicle for modifications such as changes made to wheels/tires, axle ratio, and curb height.

   Tire size: **OK** _____   **NOT OK** _____   (describe) _____

   Curb (ride) height: ___ stock ___ higher ___ lower (describe) _____

   Axle ratio: ___ stock ___ unknown (describe) _____

_____   2.   Be sure that all four tires are the same size and brand.

   LF tire size = _____   Brand = _____

   RF tire size = _____   Brand = _____

   RR tire size = _____   Brand = _____

   LR tire size = _____   Brand = _____

_____   3.   Did any of the modifications affect the braking?

   ___ **Yes**

   ___ **No** (describe) _____

_____   4.   Did the modifications set an ABS diagnostic trouble code (DTC)?

   ___ **Yes** (describe) _____

   ___ **No**

_____   5.   Check the service information and record the specified procedure to follow when servicing an antilock brake system on a vehicle that has been modified.

   _____

Pearson

We Support
ASE | Education Foundation

Traction Control/Vehicle Stability

Meets ASE Task: (A5-G-1) P-1 Identify and inspect electronic brake control system components; determine needed action.

Name _____ **Date** _____ **Time on Task** _____

Make/Model/Year _____ **VIN** _____ **Evaluation: 4 3 2 1**

_____ 1. Check service information for the specified procedure to follow when inspecting the electronic brake control system. Describe the procedure. _____

_____

_____

_____ 2. Describe the location of the following components.
  - Wheel speed sensor _____

  _____

  _____

  _____

  _____

  - Hydraulic control assembly _____

  _____

  _____

  _____

  _____

  - Other (describe)

  _____

  _____

  _____

_____ 3. Based on the inspection, what is the needed action? _____

_____

Pearson

We Support
ASE | Education Foundation

Hybrid Regenerative Brake Systems

Meets ASE Task: (A5-G-2) P-3 Describe the operation of a regenerative braking system.

Name _____ **Date** _____ **Time on Task** _____

Make/Model/Year _____ **VIN** _____ **Evaluation: 4   3   2   1**

_____ 1. Check service information to determine how a regenerative braking system operates.

Describe the operation. _____

_____

_____

_____ 2. Explain why the friction brakes last longer on a hybrid electric vehicle compared to a

conventional vehicle. _____

_____

_____

Pearson

Tire Identification

Meets ASE Task: (A4-A-2) P-1 Research applicable vehicle and service information, such as suspension and steering system operation, vehicle history, service precautions, and TSBs.

Name _____ Date _____ Time on Task _____

Make/Model/Year _____ VIN _____ Evaluation: 4 3 2 1

_____ 1. Check service information for the specified tire size(s) and inflation pressure.

Tire size = _____

Optional tire size (if specified) = _____

Spare tire size = _____

Specified tire inflation pressure = _____

_____ 2. Check the sidewall of the tires and determine the following information:

Tread wear rating = _____

Temperature resistance = _____

Traction rating = _____

Date tire was built (last four numbers of the DOT number (month/year)

= _____/_____

![Tire sidewall showing TTX0401]

Pearson

We Support

ASE | Education Foundation

Tire Pressure Monitoring System

Meets ASE Task: (A4-F-7) P-1, (A4-F-10) P-1, (A4-F-11) P-1 Inspect, diagnose and
calibrate tire pressure monitoring system.

Name _____ **Date** _____ **Time on Task** _____

Make/Model/Year _____ **VIN** _____ **Evaluation: 4   3   2   1**

_____ **1.** Check service information to determine the specified procedure to follow when
inspecting, diagnosing, or calibrating the tire pressure monitoring system. Describe
the specified procedures.

_____

_____

_____

_____ **2.** With what type of TPMS is the vehicle equipped?

   _____ Indirect

   _____ Direct

   If direct-type system, what type of
   sensor is used?

   _____ Stem-mounted

   _____ Banded

   _____ Unknown

_____ **3.** Is recalibrating the sensors needed if the tires are rotated?

   _____ Yes (If yes, what is the procedure?) _____

   _____

   _____ No

Pearson

We Support

| Education Foundation

Tire Inspection and Air Loss

Meets ASE Task: (A4-F-1) P-1, (A4-F-8) P-1 Inspect tire condition and check for loss of air pressure.

Name _____ **Date** _____ **Time on Task** _____

Make/Model/Year _____ **VIN** _____ **Evaluation:** 4 3 2 1

_____ **1.** Inspect tire condition and inflation pressure. Record the results:

	Condition	Tread Depth	Inflation Pressure
Left front	_____	_____	_____
Right front	_____	_____	_____
Right rear	_____	_____	_____
Left rear	_____	_____	_____
Spare	_____	_____	_____

_____ **2.** Check tires for air loss. Describe the procedure used. _____

_____

_____ **3.** Based on the inspection results, what is the needed action? _____

_____

_____

TIRE TREAD

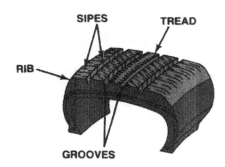

Tire Vibration and Pull Diagnosis

Meets ASE Task: (A4-F-2) P-2, (A4-F5) P-1 Diagnose vibration and pull concerns; determine needed action.

Name _____ **Date** _____ **Time on Task** _____

Make/Model/Year _____ **VIN** _____ **Evaluation: 4   3   2   1**

_____ **1.** Check service information for the specified procedures to follow when diagnosing vibration and pull concerns. Describe the recommended procedures.

_____

_____

_____ **2.** Check all that are specified:

_____ Test drive

_____ Use an electronic vibration analyzer (EVA)

_____ Visual inspection

_____ Measure radial runout _____

_____ Measure lateral runout _____

_____ Rotate tires

_____ Other (describe) _____

_____

WHEEL FLANGE

DIAL INDICATOR SUPPORT

DIAL INDICATOR

_____ **3.** Based on the diagnostic procedures, what is the needed action?

_____

_____

Pearson

Tire Rotation

Meets ASE Task: (A4-F-3) P-1 Rotate tires according to manufacturer's recommendations.

Name _____ **Date** _____ **Time on Task** _____

Make/Model/Year _____ **VIN** _____ **Evaluation: 4   3   2   1**

_____ **1.** Check the service information for the recommended tire rotation method.

    _____ Cannot rotate tires on this vehicle
    _____ Modified X method
    _____ X method
    _____ Front to rear and rear to front

_____ **2.** Hoist the vehicle safely to a good working position (chest level).

_____ **3.** Remove the wheels and rotate them (if possible) according to the vehicle manufacturer's recommendation.

_____ **4.** Check and correct the tire air pressures according to the service information on the placard on the driver's door.

    Specified front tire air pressure = _____

    Specified rear tire air pressure = _____

_____ **5.** Tighten the lug nuts to factory specifications. What is the factory specification?

    _____

_____ **6.** Lower the vehicle and move the hoist pads before driving the vehicle out of the service stall.

Pearson

We Support
ASE | Education Foundation

Tire, Wheel, Axle, and Hub Runout

Meets ASE Task: (A4-F-4) P-2 Measure wheel, tire, axle flange, and hub runout; determine needed action.

Name _____ **Date** _____ **Time on Task** _____

Make/Model/Year _____ **VIN** _____ **Evaluation: 4   3   2   1**

_____ **1.** Check service information for the specifications for radial and lateral runout.

Specification for radial runout = _____ (usually less than 0.060 inch).

Specification for lateral runout = _____ (usually less than 0.045 inch).

_____ **2.** Using a runout gauge, rotate the tire and record the radial runout (roundness of the tires) and the lateral runout (side-to-side movement) of the tires.

Tire	Radial Runout	Lateral Runout
R.F.	_____	_____
R.R.	_____	_____
L.F.	_____	_____
L.R.	_____	_____

_____ **3.** Using a dial indicator, measure the axle and hub runout.

Hub runout   = _____   OK ____   NOT OK ____

Flange runout   = _____   OK ____   NOT OK ____

CHECKING HUB RUNOUT

CHECKING MOUNTING FLANGE RUNOUT

_____ **4.** Based on the measurements, what needed action is needed?

_____

_____

Pearson

Tire Replacement

Meets ASE Task: (A4-F-6) P-1 Dismount and remount tire on wheel; balance.

Name _____   **Date** _____   **Time on Task** _____

Make/Model/Year _____   **VIN** _____   **Evaluation: 4   3   2   1**

_____ **1.** Check the instructions for the proper use of the tire changer. Describe the recommended procedure.

_____

_____

_____ **2.** Check all steps that were performed.

_____ **Removed the valve core** (TPMS equipped tire/wheel assembly; check service information for the exact procedure to follow.)

INSTALL TPMS SENSOR
FLAT SIDE DOWN

_____ **Demount the tire from the wheel. Instructor OK** _____

_____ **Clean bead seat.**

_____ **Lubricate the tire bead.**

_____ **Mount the tire and inflate** to specified inflation pressure.

_____ **3.** Balance tire/wheel assembly.

Instructor OK _____

Education Foundation

Tire Repair

Meets ASE Task: (A4-F-9) P-1 Repair tire using internal patch.

Name _____ **Date** _____ **Time on Task** _____

Make/Model/Year _____ **VIN** _____ **Evaluation: 4   3   2   1**

_____ 1. Locate the source of the leak by submerging the tire under water or by spraying the tire with soapy water. Describe the location of the leak.

_____

_____ 2. Remove the foreign object and use a reamer to clean the hole in the tire (tread area only).

_____ 3. Dismount the tire and buff the inside of the tire around the hole.

_____ 4. Apply rubber cement to the buffed area.

_____ 5. Insert the repair plug from the inside of the tire.

_____ 6. Pull the plug through the puncture from the outside of the tire.

_____ 7. Use a stitching tool to make sure the inside of the patch is well adhered to the inside of the tire.

_____ 8. Remove the tire and inflate to the air pressure specified by the vehicle manufacturer.

_____ 9. Check the repair for air leaks using soapy water.

   OK ____   NOT OK ____

Suspension and Steering System Information

Meets ASE Task: (A4-A-2) P-1 Research applicable vehicle and service information.

Name _____ **Date** _____ **Time on Task** _____

Make/Model/Year _____ **VIN** _____ **Evaluation: 4   3   2   1**

Consult the service information and determine the following.

_____ **1.** List suspension-related technician service bulletins (TSBs).

      A. Topic _____ Bulletin Number _____

         Fault/Concern _____

         Needed Action _____

      B. Topic _____ Bulletin Number _____

         Fault/Concern _____

         Needed Action _____

_____ **2.** List all published service precautions from the service information.

     _____

     _____

_____ **3.** Research the vehicle's service history and record all suspension or steering service or repairs.

     _____

     _____

_____ **4.** Record all suspension and steering specifications.

     _____

     _____

Pearson

Research Vehicle Service Information

Meets ASE Task: (A4-A-1) P-1 Research vehicle service information.

Name _____ **Date** _____ **Time on Task** _____

Make/Model/Year _____ **VIN** _____ **Evaluation: 4 3 2 1**

_____ **1.** Check service information and check the following for the vehicle being serviced.

- Power steering fluid type _____

- Technical service bulletin (list all that apply). _____

_____

_____

_____

![Honda Genuine HG Power Steering Fluid Advanced Protection. Formulated specifically for Honda and Acura vehicles. HONDA. 12 fl.oz. / 354 ml.]

- Service precautions (list all that apply). _____

_____

_____

_____

Suspension Problem Diagnosis

Meets ASE Task: (A4-A-2) P-1 Identify and interpret suspension concerns; determine needed action.

Name _____ Date _____ Time on Task _____

Make/Model/Year _____ VIN _____ Evaluation: 4 3 2 1

_____ 1. What is the stated customer concern? _____

_____ 2. Test drive the vehicle under the same conditions and road surface types as stated by the customer when the problem occurs and check the following.

Tire-type noise?   OK ____   NOT OK ____
Clunks?   OK ____   NOT OK ____
Creaks?   OK ____   NOT OK ____
Tracks straight?   OK ____   NOT OK ____
Pull during braking only?   OK ____   NOT OK ____
Wandering (unstable)?   OK ____   NOT OK ____
Other concern (describe) _____

_____ 3. When does the fault or concern occur?

____ During turns or cornering to the right
____ During turns or cornering to the left
____ During turns or cornering both to the right or the left
____ While driving straight ahead
____ Only when driving on a rough road
____ Only when turning into or out of a driveway
____ Other (describe) _____

_____ 4. Based on the test drive, what components or systems could be the cause of the suspension problem or concern?

_____

_____

_____ 5. What action will be needed to correct these concerns? _____

_____

_____

Pearson

We Support
ASE | Education Foundation

Diagnose Suspension Concerns

Meets ASE Task: (A4-C-1) P-1, (A4-C-2) P-2   Diagnose SLA and strut suspension concerns; determine needed action.

Name _____ **Date** _____ **Time on Task** _____

Make/Model/Year _____ **VIN** _____ **Evaluation: 4   3   2   1**

_____ **1.** Check service information for the specified procedures to follow when diagnosing suspension-related concerns. Check all items that are specified.

    _____ Road Test

    _____ Visual inspection

    _____ Ride height measurement

    _____ Other (describe) _____

    _____

_____ **2.** Based on the inspection, what is the needed action? _____

_____

_____

_____

We Support
ASE | Education Foundation

Suspension Inspection/Component Replacement

Meets ASE Task: (A4-C-3) P-3, (A4-C-4) P-3, (A4-C-5) P-2, (A4-C-6) P-3, (A4-C-7) P-3
Front suspension inspection and component replacement.

Name _____ **Date** _____ **Time on Task** _____

Make/Model/Year _____ **VIN** _____ **Evaluation:** 4 3 2 1

_____ **1.** Check service information for the exact procedures to follow when removing, inspecting, and replacing front suspension components. Describe the recommended procedures.

_____

_____

_____ **2.** Check all components that were inspected, removed or replaced.

_____ Upper control arms/bushings

_____ Lower control arms/bushings

_____ Strut rods/bushings

_____ Steering knuckle

_____ Coil springs and spring insulators

_____ **3.** Describe the reason why the parts were replaced. _____

_____

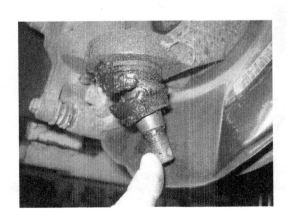

Torsion Bar

Meets ASE Task: (A4-C-8) P-3 Remove, inspect, install, and adjust suspension system torsion bars; inspect mounts.

Name _____ **Date** _____ **Time on Task** _____

Make/Model/Year _____ **VIN** _____ **Evaluation: 4   3   2   1**

_____ 1. Check the service information for the specified removal and reinstallation procedure.

_____

_____

_____

_____

_____ 2. List the tools needed.

_____

_____

_____

_____

_____

_____ 3. Check the service information and describe the proper ride height adjustment procedure.

TORSION BAR

_____

_____

_____

_____

_____

_____ 4. Inspect the torsion bar mounts.

OK _____   **NOT OK** _____

Describe the faults and needed action.

_____

_____

Pearson

Strut Rod and Stabilizer Bushings

Meets ASE Task: (A4-C-9) P-3 Inspect, test, and replace thermostat and gasket/seal.

Name _____ **Date** _____ **Time on Task** _____

Make/Model/Year _____ **VIN** _____ **Evaluation: 4   3   2   1**

_____ **1.** Check service information for the exact procedure to follow to remove, inspect, and
install struts and bushings. Describe the recommended steps.

_____

_____

_____

_____

_____

_____

_____

_____ **2.** Check service information for
the exact procedures to follow to remove, inspect, and
install stabilizer bar bushings. Describe the recommended steps.

_____

_____

MacPherson Strut Service

Meets ASE Task: (A4-C-10) P-3 Remove, inspect, and install strut cartridge or assembly, strut coil spring, insulators (silencers), and upper strut bearing mount.

Name _____ **Date** _____ **Time on Task** _____

Make/Model/Year _____ **VIN** _____ **Evaluation: 4   3   2   1**

_____ **1.** Check the service information for the specified service procedure.

_____

_____

_____

_____ **2.** Safely support the vehicle on jacks and/or the lift.

_____ **3.** Remove the upper and lower attaching bolts and nuts.

_____ **4.** Carefully remove the MacPherson strut assembly from the vehicle.

_____ **5.** Compress the coil spring with the proper equipment and replace the strut assembly.

Show the instructor the disassembled unit.

Instructor's OK _____

_____ **6.** Reinstall the complete assembly.

NOTE: The vehicle should be aligned after replacing the strut assembly.

STRUT COVER

UPPER SPRING SEAT

DUST COVER

COIL SPRING

LATERAL LINK

TRAILING LINK

Pearson

Front Shock Absorber Replacement

Meets ASE Task: (A4-D-1) P-1 Inspect, remove, and replace shock absorbers.

Name _____ **Date** _____ **Time on Task** _____

Make/Model/Year _____ **VIN** _____ **Evaluation:** 4 3 2 1

_____ **1.** Verify that the front shock absorber requires replacement. Check all that apply:

      _____ bent or damaged shock or mounting hardware
      _____ shock absorber is leaking hydraulic fluid
      _____ excessively worn - causing tire wear or riding comfort problems
      _____ other (specify) _____

_____ **2.** Compare the replacement shocks to the original shocks to be sure that they are correct.
    OK _____ **NOT OK** _____
NOTE: All shock absorbers should be replaced in pairs only. Do not replace just one shock absorber.

_____ **3.** Check the service information for the specified replacement procedure. _____
_____
_____

HINT: Many shocks on rear-wheel-drive vehicles can be broken off using a deep-well socket and a long extension. By rocking the extension back and forth, the top of the shock will usually break off saving the time and effort it takes to remove a nut that is often rusted in place after many years of service.

_____ **4.** Safely hoist the vehicle.

_____ **5.** Remove the lower shock absorber retaining bolts (nuts) as per the service information instructions..

CAUTION: Be ready to catch the shock absorber because it will likely fall after removing the last retaining bolt (nut).

_____ **6.** Show the instructor the removed shock absorber. **Instructor's OK** _____

_____ **7.** Extend the rod on the replacement shock and install the lower retaining bolts (nuts).

_____ **8.** Lower the vehicle and install the upper retaining fastener.

_____ **9.** Bounce the vehicle to check that the replacement shock does not interfere with any part of the suspension or frame.

_____ **10.** Test drive the vehicle before returning it to the customer.

Pearson

We Support
ASE | Education Foundation

Shock Absorber/Strut Cartridge Replacement

Meets ASE Task: (A4-C-10) P-3 Inspect, test, and replace thermostat and gasket/seal.

Name _____ **Date** _____ **Time on Task** _____

Make/Model/Year _____ **VIN** _____ **Evaluation: 4   3   2   1**

_____ **1.** Check service information for the specified procedure to follow when inspecting, removing, and replacing shock absorbers. Describe recommended steps.

_____

_____

_____ **2.** Instructor OK after removal

_____

_____ **3.** Check service information for the specified procedures to follow when inspecting, removing, and replacing strut cartridges. Describe the recommended steps.

_____

_____

_____

_____

_____ **4.** Instructors OK after removal _____

Pearson

Rear Leaf Springs

Meets ASE Task: (A4-C-12) P-1 Remove, inspect, and install leaf springs, leaf spring insulators (silencers), shackles, brackets, bushings, and mounts.

Name _____ **Date** _____ **Time on Task** _____

Make/Model/Year _____ **VIN** _____ **Evaluation: 4   3   2   1**

_____ **1.** Check the service information for the specified procedure for the removal and reinstallation of rear leaf springs.

_____

_____

_____

_____ **2.** List the tools and equipment needed. _____

_____

_____ **3.** Show the instructor the removed rear leaf spring(s). **Instructor's OK** _____

_____ **4.** List the tightening torque specifications for the affected fasteners. _____

_____

We Support
Education Foundation

Inspect, Remove, or Replace Suspension Components

Meets ASE Task: (A4-C-11) P-3 Inspect, remove and/or replace track bar, strut rods/radius arms.

Name _____ Date _____ Time on Task _____

Make/Model/Year _____ VIN _____ Evaluation: 4 3 2 1

_____ 1. Check service information for the specified procedure to follow when inspecting and replacing track bar and/or strut rods. Describe the specified procedure.

_____

_____

_____

_____ 2. Describe the location of the track bar (if equipped). _____

_____

_____

_____ 3. Describe the location of the strut rods/radius arms (if equipped). _____

_____

_____

Electronic Suspension Diagnosis

Meets ASE Task: (A4-D-3) P-3 Test and diagnose components of electronically controlled
suspension systems using a scan tool; determine needed action.

Name _____ **Date** _____ **Time on Task** _____

Make/Model/Year _____ **VIN** _____ **Evaluation: 4   3   2   1**

_____ 1. Check the service information and determine the specified testing procedures.

_____

_____

_____

_____ 2. Check the service information and compare normal scan tool readings of the
electronically controlled suspension system to the actual readings obtained from the
vehicle.

Parameter	Normal Reading	Actual Reading
_____	_____	_____
_____	_____	_____
_____	_____	_____
_____	_____	_____
_____	_____	_____
_____	_____	_____
_____	_____	_____
_____	_____	_____

_____ 3. Based on the service information and the scan tool data, what is the needed action?

_____

_____

_____

Airbag System and Steering Wheel Service

Meets ASE Task: (A4-B-1) P-1, (A4-B-2) P-1 Disable and enable airbag system and center/replace the clockspring.

Name _____ **Date** _____ **Time on Task** _____

Make/Model/Year _____ **VIN** _____ **Evaluation: 4 3 2 1**

_____ **1.** Check service information for the specified procedures to follow when disabling an airbag system. Check all that apply.

    _____ Disconnect the negative battery cable.

    _____ Remove the airbag fuse.

    _____ Disconnect the electrical connector(s)

    _____ Other (describe) _____

_____ **2.** Check service information for the specified procedure to follow when removing and replacing the steering wheel. Describe the recommended procedures.

_____

_____

_____ **3.** Describe the specified method to center the airbag system clockspring.

_____

Pearson

Steering Column Related Diagnosis

Meets ASE Task: (A4-B-3) P-2, (A4-B-6) P-2 Steering column inspection and diagnosis; determine needed action.

Name _____ **Date** _____ **Time on Task** _____

Make/Model/Year _____ **VIN** _____ **Evaluation: 4   3   2   1**

_____ 1. Check service information for the specified procedures to follow when diagnosing a conventional steering gear. Describe recommended procedures.

_____

_____

_____ 2. Check service information for the specified procedures for checking the following steering components.

_____ Universal joint - _____

_____ Flexible coupling - _____

_____ Collapsible column - _____

_____ Lock cylinder - _____

_____ Steering wheel - _____

_____ 3. Based on the results of the inspection, what is the needed action? _____

_____

_____

Pearson

We Support
ASE | Education Foundation

Steering Gear Adjustment and Replacement

Meets ASE Task: (A4-B-7) P-2 Adjust non-rack and pinion worm bearing preload and sector lash; Remove and replace rack and pinion steering gear.

Name _____ **Date** _____ **Time on Task** _____

Make/Model/Year _____ **VIN** _____ **Evaluation: 4   3   2   1**

_____ **1.** Check service information for the specified procedure to follow to adjust a conventional steering gear assembly Describe the recommended procedure for:

Worm bearing preload - _____

_____

Sector lash (overcenter adjustment) - _____

_____

_____ **2.** Check service information for the specified procedure to follow for replacing a rack and pinion steering gear assembly. Describe the recommended procedures.

_____

_____

_____ **3.** Describe the condition of the mounting bushings and brackets. _____

_____

We Support
ASE | Education Foundation

Steering Problem Diagnosis

Meets ASE Task: (A4-A-2) P-1 Identify and interpret steering concerns; determine needed action.

_____

Name _____ **Date** _____ **Time on Task** _____

Make/Model/Year _____ **VIN** _____ **Evaluation: 4   3   2   1**

_____ 1. What is the stated customer concern? _____

_____ 2. Test drive the vehicle under the same condition and road surface types as stated by the customer when the problem occurs and check the following.

Steers straight?	OK ____	NOT OK ____
Wanders?	OK ____	NOT OK ____
Noise during turns or corners?	OK ____	NOT OK ____
Hard steering when cold only?	OK ____	NOT OK ____
Hard steering when raining?	OK ____	NOT OK ____
Noise when steering?	OK ____	NOT OK ____
Looseness in steering wheel?	OK ____	NOT OK ____
Lack of steering control?	OK ____	NOT OK ____

Other concerns (describe) _____

_____

_____ 3. When does the fault or concern occur?

____ During turns or cornering to the right
____ During turns or cornering to the left
____ During turns or cornering both to the right or the left
____ While driving straight ahead
____ Only when driving on a rough road
____ Only when turning into or out of a driveway
____ Other (describe) _____

_____ 4. Based on the test drive, what components or systems could be the cause of the suspension problem or concern?

_____

_____

_____ 5. What action will be needed to correct these concerns? _____

_____

_____

Pearson

Education Foundation

Inner Tie Rod Ends and Bellows Boots

Meets ASE Task: (A4-B-8) P-1 Inspect and replace rack and pinion steering gear inner tie ends (sockets) and bellows boots.

Name _____ Date _____ Time on Task _____

Make/Model/Year _____ VIN _____ Evaluation: 4 3 2 1

_____ 1. Check the service information and write the specified procedure to inspect and replace the inner tie rod ends.

_____

_____

_____

_____

_____ 2. Hoist the vehicle safely and visually check the condition of the inner tie rod end bellows boots.

  _____ OK
  _____ Cracked in places, but not all the way through (recommend replacement)
  _____ Cracked open places (requires replacement)
  _____ Missing

_____ 3. Most vehicle manufacturers recommend that the entire rack and pinion steering gear assembly be removed from the vehicle when replacing the inner tie rod ends (ball socket assemblies).

  _____ **Yes** (recommend that rack be removed)
  _____ **No** (the tie rod end can be removed with the rack in the vehicle)

_____ 4. Describe the method used to retain the inner ball sockets to the ends of the rack.

  _____ Pin
  _____ Rivet
  _____ Stacked
  _____ Other (describe) _____

_____ 5. List all precautions found in the service information regarding this procedure.

_____

_____ 6. Describe any problems _____

Pearson

Inspect and Replace Steering Components

Meets ASE Task: (A4-B-16) P-2, (A4-C-6) P-3 Inspect and replace pitman arm, relay (centerlink/intermediate) rod, idler arm and mountings, and steering linkage damper.

Name _____ **Date** _____ **Time on Task** _____

Make/Model/Year _____ **VIN** _____ **Evaluation: 4   3   2   1**

_____ 1. Check the service information for the specified testing and inspection procedures and specifications.

A. Specified testing procedures: _____

_____

B. Specifications: _____

_____

_____ 2. Check the steering components listed and note their condition.

Idler arm: _____

_____

Pitman arm: _____

_____

Centerlink: _____

_____

Steering linkage damper: _____

_____

DIAL INDICATOR

MEASURE PLAY

IDLER ARM

SPRING SCALE

_____ 3. State the specified replacement procedure and list any specific tools needed.

Idler arm: Procedure _____

Tools _____

Pitman arm: Procedure _____

Tools _____

Centerlink: Procedure _____

Tools _____

Steering linkage damper: Procedure _____

Tools _____

Tie-Rod End Inspection and Replacement

Meets ASE Task: (A4-B-17) P-1 Inspect, replace, and adjust tie rod ends (sockets), tie rod sleeves and clamps.

Name _____ **Date** _____ **Time on Task** _____

Make/Model/Year _____ **VIN** _____ **Evaluation: 4   3   2   1**

_____ **1.** Verify that the tie-rod end(s) requires replacement. Check all that apply.

       _____ Torn boot
       _____ Joint has side-to-side movement
       _____ Physically damaged
       _____ Other (specify) _____

_____ **2.** Hoist the vehicle safely.

_____ **3.** Compare the replacement tie-rod end with the original to be sure that the new end is correct.

_____ **4.** Remove the retaining nut and use a tie-rod puller to separate the tie-rod end from the steering knuckle and/or center link.

HINT: Often a hammer can be used to jar loose the tie-rod end especially if a downward force is exerted on the tie-rod while an assistant taps on the steering knuckle at the tie-rod end.

_____ **5.** Measure the distance between the center of the tie-rod end and the adjusting sleeve and record this distance so the replacement tie-rod end can be installed in approximately the same location so that the wheel alignment (toe setting) will be close to being correct.

_____ **6.** Unscrew the old tie-rod end and discard.

_____ **7.** Install the replacement tie-rod end and adjust to the same distance as measured and recorded in #5.

_____ **8.** Install the tie-rod end onto the steering knuckle and torque the retaining nut to factory specifications.

       Torque specifications for the tie-rod retaining nut = _____

_____ **9.** Lower the vehicle and align the vehicle before returning it to the customer.

Pearson

Steering Gear Diagnosis

Meets ASE Task: (A4-B-4) P-2, (A4-B-5) P-2 Diagnose conventional and rack and pinion steering gears; determine needed action.

Name _____ **Date** _____ **Time on Task** _____

Make/Model/Year _____ **VIN** _____ **Evaluation:** 4 3 2 1

_____ **1.** Check service information for the specified procedure to follow when diagnosing conventional steering gear mechanical and noise concerns. Describe the recommended procedures.

_____

_____

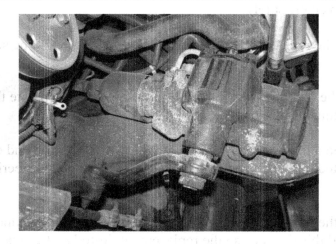

_____ **2.** Check service information for the specified procedures to follow when diagnosing a rack and pinion steering gear assembly. Describe the recommended procedures.

_____

_____

_____

_____ **3.** Based on the diagnosis, what is the needed action?

_____

We Support

Education Foundation

Power Steering Fluid

Meets ASE Task: (A4-B-9) P-1, (A4-B-10) P-2   Determine proper fluid and flush power steering system.

Name _____ **Date** _____ **Time on Task** _____

Make/Model/Year _____ **VIN** _____ **Evaluation: 4   3   2   1**

_____ **1.** Check service information for the specified fluid to use in the power steering system.

Specified fluid = _____

![Honda Genuine HG Power Steering Fluid bottle]

_____ **2.** Check service information for the specified procedure to follow when flushing, filling, and bleeding a power steering system. List the recommended steps:

Step 1 _____

Step 2 _____

Step 3 _____

Step 4 _____

Pearson

Diagnose Power Steering Fluid Leakage

Meets ASE Task: (A4-B-11) P-1 Diagnose power steering fluid leakage; determine needed action.

Name _____ Date _____ Time on Task _____

Make/Model/Year _____ VIN _____ Evaluation: 4 3 2 1

_____ 1. Check the service information for the specified power steering fluid.

    _____ Power steering fluid

    _____ Dexron III ATF

    _____ Type F ATF

    _____ Other (specify) _____

_____ 2. Perform a visual inspection of the power steering system and determine the location of any leaks. Hoist the vehicle if needed. Check each area listed below that is found to be leaking.

    _____ Pump shaft seal area

    _____ Reservoir cap

    _____ Reservoir

    _____ High-pressure line at the pump

    _____ High-pressure line between the pump and the gear

    _____ High-pressure line at the gear

    _____ Steering gear leak near the stub shaft

    _____ Steering gear leak at the inner tie rod end boots

    _____ Low-pressure hose leak (describe the location) _____

    _____ Other (describe) _____

_____ 3. What action is needed to correct the leak(s)? _____

_____

_____

_____

Power Steering Pump Belt

Meets ASE Task: (A4-B-12) P-1 Remove, inspect, replace and/or adjust power steering
pump drive belt.

Name _____ **Date** _____ **Time on Task** _____

Make/Model/Year _____ **VIN** _____ **Evaluation: 4   3   2   1**

_____ **1.** Check service information for the specified procedure and specifications when
inspecting, replacing, and/or adjusting the power steering pump drive belt. Describe
the specified procedure. _____
_____
_____

_____ **2.** How many grooves on the pulley belt: _____

_____ **3.** Does the power steering pump drive belt use a tensioner? ____ Yes ____No

If yes, does service information specify a tension test procedure?

_____
_____
_____

Service Power Steering Pump

Meets ASE Task: (A4-B-13) P-1, (A4-B-14) P-2 Remove, inspect, replace, and adjust power steering pump belt and pump; press fit pump pulley.

Name _____ **Date** _____ **Time on Task** _____

Make/Model/Year _____ **VIN** _____ **Evaluation: 4 3 2 1**

_____ **1.** Check service information for the specified procedures and specifications for removing, replacing, and adjusting the power steering pump and drive belt. Describe the recommended procedure.

_____

_____

Specified belt tension = _____

_____ **2.** Remove and reinstall power steering pump assembly.   Instructor check _____

_____ **3.** Check service information for the specified procedure to follow to remove and reinstall the power steering pump drive pulley. Describe the recommended procedure.

_____

_____

List the tools required. _____

Instructor check _____

Inspect Power Steering Hoses and Fittings

Meets ASE Task: (A4-B-15) P-2 Inspect and replace power steering hoses and fittings.

Name _____ **Date** _____ **Time on Task** _____

Make/Model/Year _____ **VIN** _____ **Evaluation: 4 3 2 1**

_____ **1.** Check the service information for the specified procedures, precautions, and torque specifications.

   A. Specified procedure: _____

   _____

   B. Specified precautions: _____

   _____

   C. Specified torque specifications _____

   _____

_____ **2.** Check the reason why the hoses and/or fittings are being replaced.

   _____ Leaking

   _____ Worn outside cover

   _____ Possible restriction as determined by testing

   _____ Recommended when replacing pump or gear assembly

   _____ Other (specify) _____

   _____

_____ **3.** Which hose(s) or fitting(s) was replaced?

   _____ High-pressure hose and fitting

   _____ Low-pressure hose and fitting

   _____ Other (specify) _____

   _____

Pearson

Power Steering System Pressure Test

Meets ASE Task: (A4-B-20) P-2 Test the power steering system pressure.

Name _____ **Date** _____ **Time on Task** _____

Make/Model/Year _____ **VIN** _____ **Evaluation: 4   3   2   1**

_____ **1.** Check service information and determine what tools and equipment are needed to check power steering system pressure. List the tools/equipment needs. _____
_____
_____
_____

_____ **2.** What is the specified procedure? Describe: _____
_____
_____

_____ **3.** What is the pressure specification? _____

_____ **4.** What were the test results? _____
_____

_____ **5.** Based on the test results, what is the needed action? _____
_____
_____

Pearson

Electronically Controlled Steering Systems

Meets ASE Task: (A4-B-18) P-2 Diagnose, test and diagnose components of electronically controlled steering systems using a scan tool.

Name _____ Date _____ Time on Task _____

Make/Model/Year _____ VIN _____ Evaluation: 4   3   2   1

_____ **1.** Check service information for the specified procedures to follow when using a scan tool to diagnose components of the electronically controlled steering system. Describe the recommended procedure.

_____

_____

_____ **2.** What components or sensors are displayed on the scan tool that are related to the electronically controlled steering system?

_____   _____

_____   _____

_____ **3.** Check service information for the specified procedures to follow when replacing components of the electronically controlled steering system. List the replaceable components and describe the specified procedures.

Replaceable components: _____

_____

Specified procedures: _____

_____

_____ **4.** What is the purpose of the idle speed compensation switch used on some vehicles?

_____

HEV Power Steering Circuits Services

Meets ASE Task: (A4-B-19) P-2 Identify hybrid vehicle power steering system electrical circuits, service, and safety precautions.

Name _____ **Date** _____ **Time on Task** _____

Make/Model/Year _____ **VIN** _____ **Evaluation: 4   3   2   1**

_____ **1.** Check service information for the specified service and safety precautions regarding the electric power steering system electrical circuits used on hybrid electric vehicles.

_____

_____

_____

_____ **2.** The electric power steering has how many volts sent to the steering gear assembly?

____ 12 volts

____ 36 volts

____ Other (specify) _____

_____ **3.** What color is the electrical conduit around the wiring to the electric power steering assembly?

____ Black

____ Yellow

____ Blue

____ Other (specify) _____

_____ **4.** List all of the safety precautions specified by the vehicle manufacturer.

_____

_____

_____

Pearson

CV Joint Noise and Vibration Diagnosis

Meets ASE Task: (A3-D-1) P-2, (A3-D-2) P-2, (A3-D-5) P-2 Diagnose constant-velocity (CV) joint noise and vibration concerns; determine needed action.

Name _____ Date _____ Time on Task _____

Make/Model/Year _____ VIN _____ Evaluation: 4 3 2 1

_____ 1. Check service information for the specified procedure that should be followed when diagnosing CV joint noise and/or vibration concerns.

_____

_____

_____ 2. Check all that were specified:

___ Drive backward while turning ___ Drive in a circle to the left and right

___ Drive forward while turning ___ Drive at highway speed

___ Drive forward straight ahead ___ Drive in reverse straight ahead

___ Other (specify) _____

_____ 3. Most vehicle manufacturers specify that the engine and transmission/transaxle mounts be checked for damage or wear. What are the conditions of the mounts?

_____

_____ 4. Based on the inspection and testing, what is the needed action? _____

_____

Pearson

U-Joint and CV Joint Service

Meets ASE Task: (A3-E-3.2) P-1, (A3-E-3.3) P-2, (A3-E-3.4) P-2, (A3-E-3.5) P-2 Inspect, service, and replace shafts, shaft center support bearings yokes, boots, and CV joints; check shaft balance and phasing.

Name _____ Date _____ Time on Task _____

Make/Model/Year _____ VIN _____ Evaluation: 4 3 2 1

_____ **1.** Check service information and determine the specified procedures, tools, and torque specification needed to service CV joints.

Specified procedure: _____

_____

Tools/equipment: _____

_____

Torque specification: _____

_____ **2.** Following the specified procedure, remove the drive axle shaft assembly.

Instructor's check _____

_____ **3.** Following the specified installation procedure, check all that were replaced.

___ Drive axle shaft assembly   ___ CV joint and boot

___ CV joint boot only   ___ Other (specify) _____

_____ **4.** Reinstall the drive axle shaft assembly.

Instructor's OK _____

We Support
ASE | Education Foundation

Pearson

Drive Axle Shaft Service

Meets ASE Task: (A3-E-3.2) P-2, (A3-D-4) P-1 Remove and replace drive axle shafts.

Name _____ **Date** _____ **Time on Task** _____

Make/Model/Year _____ **VIN** _____ **Evaluation:** 4 3 2 1

_____ **1.** Check service information for the specified procedure to follow when inspecting and
replacing drive axle shafts. Describe specified procedure. _____

_____

_____

_____ **2.** List the tools required. Check all that apply:

_____ Lug nut wrench

_____ Torque wrench

_____ Spindle nut socket

_____ CV boot protector

_____ Axle puller

_____ Other (describe) _____

_____

_____ **3.** Inspect bearings, seals, and retainers. _____

_____ **4.** Measure drive axle flange runout. What is the needed action? _____

_____

_____

Drive Axle Shaft Wheel Studs

Meets ASE Task: (A3-E-3.1) P-1 Inspect and replace drive axle shaft wheel studs.

Name _____ **Date** _____ **Time on Task** _____

Make/Model/Year _____ **VIN** _____ **Evaluation: 4 3 2 1**

_____ **1.** Check service information for the specified procedure to follow when inspecting and replacing drive axle shaft wheel studs. Describe the specified procedure. _____

_____

_____

_____

_____ **2.** What tools or equipment are needed? List the specified tools.

    1. _____

    2. _____

    3. _____

    4. _____

    5. _____

We Support

Alignment Specification

Meets ASE Task: (A4-E-2) P-1 Research applicable vehicle and service information, such as suspension and steering system operation, vehicle history, and TSBs.

Name _____   Date _____   Time on Task _____

Make/Model/Year _____   VIN _____   Evaluation: 4 3 2 1

_____ **1.** Find the following alignment angle specifications for your vehicle:

   Camber (left) preferred = _____   minimum _____   maximum _____

   Camber (right) preferred = _____   minimum _____   maximum _____

   Caster (left)   preferred = _____   minimum _____   maximum _____

   Caster (right) preferred = _____   minimum _____   maximum _____

   Front toe   preferred = _____   minimum _____   maximum _____

   Rear camber   preferred = _____   minimum _____   maximum _____

   Total rear toe preferred = _____   minimum _____   maximum _____

_____ **2.** Determine the diagnostic angle specifications for your vehicle:

   Toe-out on turn (TOOT) inside wheel = _____ degrees

                            outside wheel = _____ degrees

   Maximum allowable variation = _____ degrees

   Steering axis inclination (SAI)   left = _____

                                        right = _____

   Maximum allowable difference = _____

Pre-Alignment Inspection

Meets ASE Task: (A4-E-2) P-1 Perform prealignment inspection and measure vehicle ride height; perform needed action.

Name _____   **Date** _____   **Time on Task** _____

Make/Model/Year _____   **VIN** _____   **Evaluation: 4   3   2   1**

_____ **1.** Check tires. Both front tires and both rear tires should be checked for the following:

    A. Correct tire pressure

    B. Same size and brand

    C. Same tread depth

    OK _____   **NOT OK** _____

_____ **2.** Perform a dry-park test to check for any looseness in the steering and suspension components such as:

    A. Tie rods

    B. Idler arms

    C. Ball-joints

    D. Control arm bushings

    E. Loose or defective wheel bearings

    OK _____   **NOT OK** _____

_____ **3.** Check for proper ride height.

    A. Front and rear

    B. Left and right

    OK _____   **NOT OK** _____

We Support

Education Foundation

Diagnose Alignment-Related Faults

Meets ASE Task: (A4-E-1) P-1 Diagnose vehicle wander, drift, pull, bump steer, and torque steer.

Name _____ **Date** _____ **Time on Task** _____

Make/Model/Year _____ **VIN** _____ **Evaluation:** 4 3 2 1

_____ **1.** Check service information for the specified procedure to follow when diagnosing drift, pull, or wander. Describe the specified procedure. _____

_____

_____

_____ **2.** Check service information for the specified procedure to follow when diagnosing bump steer. Describe the specified procedure. _____

_____

_____

_____ **3.** Check service information for the specified procedure to follow when diagnosing memory steer. Describe the specified procedure. _____

_____

_____

_____ **4.** Check service information for the specified procedure to follow when diagnosing torque steer and steering return concerns. Describe the specified procedure. _____

_____

_____

_____ **5.** Based on the tests and procedures performed, what is the needed action? _____

_____

_____

Alignment Angle Readings

Meets ASE Task: (A4-E-3) P-1 Prepare vehicle for wheel alignment on the alignment machine; perform four-wheel alignment by checking and adjusting wheel caster.

Name _____ **Date** _____ **Time on Task** _____

Make/Model/Year _____ **VIN** _____ **Evaluation: 4 3 2 1**

_____ **1.** Hoist the vehicle on the alignment rack and install the wheel sensors.

_____ **2.** Compensate the wheel sensors as per the alignment equipment manufacturer's recommended procedure.

_____ **3.** Lower the vehicle and jounce (bounce) to center the suspension.

_____ **4.** Read the rear camber and toe.

	LR	RR
Camber	_____	_____
Toe	_____	_____

Total rear toe = _____

_____ **5.** Read the front camber and toe.

	LF	RF
Camber	_____	_____
Toe	_____	_____

Total front toe = _____

_____ **6.** Perform a caster sweep to determine the front caster and SAI.

	LF	RF
Caster	_____	_____
SAI	_____	_____

Describe what (if anything) is wrong with the present alignment.

_____

Pearson

TOOT and SAI

Meets ASE Task: (A4-E-4) P-2, (A4-E-5) P-2   Check toe-out-on-turns (turning radius) and SAI (steering axis inclination) and included angle; determine needed action.

Name _____ **Date** _____ **Time on Task** _____

Make/Model/Year _____ **VIN** _____ **Evaluation: 4   3   2   1**

_____ **1.** Check the alignment equipment instructions and measure the toe-out-on-turns.

        LEFT TOOT   **RIGHT TOOT**

        _____   _____

_____ **2.** Check service information for the specified toe-out-on-turns (TOOT).

        Specifications = _____

_____ **3.** Based on the TOOT readings, what is the needed action?

        _____

        _____

_____ **4.** Check steering axis inclination (SAI) and compare to factory specifications.

        SAI LEFT   **SAI RIGHT**

        _____   _____

        Specification for SAI = _____

_____ **5.** Based on the SAI reading, what is the needed action?

        _____

        _____

        _____

Four-Wheel Alignment

Meets ASE Task: (A4-E-6) P-1, (A4-E-9) P-2 Prepare vehicle for wheel alignment on the alignment machine; perform four-wheel alignment by checking and adjusting wheel caster.

Name _____ Date _____ Time on Task _____

Make/Model/Year _____ VIN _____ Evaluation: 4 3 2 1

Specifications:

	Left	Right
Camber	_____	_____
Caster	_____	_____
Toe (Total)	_____	
KPI/SAI	_____	
Rear Camber	_____	_____
Rear Toe	_____	_____
Rear Toe (Total)	_____	

Methods of Adjustment:

	Front	Rear
Camber	_____	_____
Caster	_____	
Toe	_____	_____

Reading Before Alignment: (Record here and attach the print out.)

	Left	Right
Camber	_____	_____
Caster	_____	_____
Toe (Total)	_____	
KPI/SAI	_____	
Rear Camber	_____	_____
Rear Toe	_____	
Thrust	_____	
Set Back	_____	

Reading After Alignment: (Record here and attach the print out.)

	Left	Right
Camber	_____	_____
Caster	_____	_____
Toe (Total)	_____	
KPI/SAI	_____	
Rear Camber	_____	_____
Rear Toe	_____	
Thrust	_____	
Set Back	_____	

Diagnostic Alignment Angles

Meets ASE Task: (A4-E-7) P-2, (A4-E-8) P-3 Check angles that can detect collision damage; determine needed action.

Name _____ **Date** _____ **Time on Task** _____

Make/Model/Year _____ **VIN** _____ **Evaluation: 4   3   2   1**

_____ **1.** Measure the rear thrust angle and compare it to factory specifications.

Measured rear thrust angle = _____

Specified thrust angle = _____

_____ **2.** Based on the results of the rear thrust angle measurement, what is the needed action.?

_____

_____

_____ **3.** Measure the front wheel setback and compare it to factory specifications.

Measured front wheel setback = _____

Specified front wheel setback = _____

_____ **4.** Based on the results of the front wheel setback measurement, what is the needed action.?

_____

_____

_____ **5.** Check service information for the specified location and dimensions to check for the proper alignment of the front and/or rear cradle (subframe).

_____

_____

_____ **6.** Based on the results of the measurements, compared to factory specifications, what is the needed action?

_____

Pearson

Noise and Vibration Diagnosis

Meets ASE Task: (A3-D-5) P-2, (A4-A-1) P-1, (A4-D-5) P-2 Diagnose wheel/tire vibration, shimmy, and noise; determine needed action.

Name _____ Date _____ Time on Task _____

Make/Model/Year _____ VIN _____ Evaluation: 4   3   2   1

_____ **1.** Check service information for the specified (if any) methods and procedures to follow when diagnosing noise and/or vibration concerns.

_____

_____

_____ **2.** Test drive the vehicle and verify the concerns. Check all that apply:

___ Noise   ___ Vibration   ___ Both

_____ **3.** If there is a vibration, what frequency and at what speed is the vibration?

Frequency _____   Vehicle speed _____

Frequency _____   Vehicle speed _____

Frequency _____   Vehicle speed _____

Frequency _____   Vehicle speed _____

_____ **4.** If a noise, check for witness marks and describe this location: _____

_____

_____ **5.** Based on the test results and visual inspection, what is the needed action?

_____